LINGERING AT CALVARY

Lingering at Calvary

BY S. FRANKLIN LOGSDON

© Copyright 1981

by Bible Memory Association International

Bible Memory Association
International
P. O. Box 12,000, St. Louis, Missouri 63112

ISBN 0-89323-025-1

*To Him Whom having not seen
we love; in Whom, though now
we see Him not, yet believing,
we rejoice with joy unspeakable
and full of glory.*

FOREWORD . . .

By V. Raymond Edman
President, Wheaton College

OUR EARTH has many entrancing and awe-inspiring eminences that stretch heaven-ward far above the lowlands and marshes—Everest in the Himalayas, Chimborazo along the Equator in South America and Kenya in Africa, the Matterhorn and Jungfrau in the Swiss Alps, and McKinley and Aconcagua at opposite ends of the long cordillera of the Americas. Among the high places of earth Calvary is geographically insignificant and inconsequential, but spiritually it is the loftiest of all, for thereon was the redemption of the human heart made possible by the sacrifice of the Saviour.

With Pastor Logsdon we climb the slow and painful ascent of the *Via Dolorosa* to the summit of Calvary, there to view anew the scene of our Lord's suffering, shame and death; and we linger at Calvary because we love Him, to reflect upon the statements of Holy Writ about Him. What did the prophet mean by saying, "It pleased the Lord to bruise him?" or "He shall see of the travail of his soul and shall be satisfied?" Why was He "numbered among the transgressors" and how shall He "prolong his days?"

A hasty glance at Calvary will not suffice to kindle our hearts nor to enlighten our minds, but lingering there will help. Thereby we shall begin to comprehend here on earth something of our song in ages to come—"Unto him who loved us and washed us from our sins in his own blood."

AUTHOR'S PREFACE . . .

ANY APPROACH TO CALVARY is a sacred venture. We should take the shoes from off our feet, for the ground upon which we stand is holy. No one at any time has ascended to the highest summit of divine revelation as it gathers round this peak of perfect sacrifice, but weak men are made strong as they travel the trails of truth to this holy spot. Hearts are purified; thoughts are cleansed; devotion is enhanced.

Calvary is the focal point of prophecy; it is also the vantage point for the prophet. He who plants his feet here by faith has a deeper, truer, richer sense of spiritual values. He at once is constrained by the outlook and concerned by the inlook. Impurity, unforgiveness and indifference cannot flourish in the atmosphere of the cross any more than malignancy can flourish in healthy tissue. At the cross all argument ceases, self-justification vanishes and arrogant pride is slain utterly.

When Moses stood on the mountain peak of Genesis three-fifteen and promulgated the prophecy of the serpent versus the seed of the woman, little did he realize that the extreme end of that crimson cord would fasten to a rocky crest and coil around a rugged cross. Such however was the case. When the fulness of time was come, God sent forth His Son Who left the ivory palaces, put aside His royal wardrobe that smelled of aloes and myrrh,[1] and came into this world of sin, sorrow and shame. In due course, He was led by those whom He had come to lead, and they came to the place called Calvary. There, the Scriptures pointedly declare, they crucified Him.

[1]Ps. 45:8.

In the blueprints of omniscience, ere the world began, Calvary was pin-pointed in the topography of the holy land. The details were minutely mapped out. They were inevitable of fulfilment. Jesus affirmed at the last supper, "The Son of man goeth as it is written of him." The *Via Dolorosa* was but part of the course which the Saviour must needs traverse in order to bring many sons unto the Father, but the Place of the Skull was the climax of ignominy.

Although the word *Calvary* does not appear in the original manuscripts, it has become one of those universally accepted and generally appreciated interpolations which would now create an irreparable loss by its absence from our biblical vocabulary. Hymn writers have drawn upon it freely for devotional suggestion which suffuses the soul with the glory of sentiment. Theologians, too, have employed it with frequency and without apology as synonymous with the work of redemption which our Saviour so gloriously and so completely accomplished on Golgotha's blood-stained brow.

A GLIMPSE OF CALVARY...

In thought we journey to the place where He,
The Christ of God arrived so willingly—
The gracious Lamb without a spot, arose
Amid the taunts and wicked glee of those
He came to lead to life anew; but they
Led Him, and brought Him to the Skull that day.

'Tis more than just a story told, so true,
So tender, how His love unfolds, for you,
For me. But how can human words relate
The truth that He one day without the gate
Went forth to die and suffer there disgrace,
That all mankind might know His saving grace?

But let not darkness as a shroud eclipse
The truth which issued from His blessed lips:
"The Son of man is come," He said, "to die."
Nor need we in our musings ask Him why;
For we without a single hope had died
Had Jesus not that day been crucified.

The place to which we come, so gruesome—cold,
Is where the pangs of hell on Him got hold;
The pangs which might have in their firm embrace
Held us eternally had not His grace
The fetters broken, bringing sweet release;
And sweeter still the blessings of His peace.

We plant our feet by faith on this blest mount
And all our blessings o'er we feign would count
But cannot. Then by faith's clear eye we see
In truth the wonders of blest Calvary.
How great it was and good that He should go
And take my guilt and carry all my woe.

But now it's placed on yonder brow, that tree,
Between two thieves where all the throng can see
The shame. No wonder that the sun went dim,
At once short-circuited because of Him—
So luminous with holy light and love—
Pierced through with darts so fierce, beneath, above.

No wonder too that mother earth did quake
And made the rocks upon her breast to break:
The day had come when from that place of shame,
Hope should be born, and in that matchless Name,
All men of earth in passing time should see
The marvels of Christ's work on Calvary.

CONTENTS

The Place of Perfidy

"And when they were come to the place which is called Calvary, there they crucified him"—Luke 23:33.

LINGERING AT CALVARY furnishes the believer with an increasing desire to penetrate deeper into the mysteries of the Cross. And this leads one deeper into the very heart of God. No ordinary advancement this! We ought to tread softly. Reverence should subdue our souls; the fragrance of prayer should permeate our spirits; while our eyes should be opened by the Divine Illuminator to behold wondrous things.

Calvary is luminous with love and mercy. They co-mingle in a voluntary, substitutional act, on the part of the Saviour, for those who otherwise had not a single vestige of hope. The *Skull* is the monumental point where God *forever* settled the matter of satanic domination and sealed the doom of him who so disastrously deceived the nations. At the same time, He there provided a safe and secure refuge for faith-exercising folk of all ages. Calvary is the *Mecca* for devoted hearts, but it is not a physical shrine to which deluded pilgrims journey in the hope of finding mysterious power to alleviate personal afflictions. No, it is greater than that and more meaningful. It is the divine means whereby destitute men, through faith, contact elevating power and rise to hope and happy expectation. Calvary is more than the lighthouse for sinking souls; it is the lifeline for their salvation.

The exactions were unspeakable. Our blessed Saviour met treason, treachery and shame. Take a look at Simon of Cyrene, for instance. Analyze his objections when he was required to assist Jesus in bearing the cross. His trip from Tripoli was expressly for the purpose of fulfilling the ceremonial demands of the Jewish law. He had come to worship. He was a devout man and sincere. Any attachment to the cross, even to laying a finger upon it, would quickly disqualify him for worship and would at once invalidate his every dedicated effort. It would render him unclean. He would be associated with malefactors and would then be subjected to the vituperation vented by the motley crowds along the course. He immediately shrank from any such involvement, but all protests were unavailing. They compelled him. If Simon thought himself holy by virtue of his preparation for some ceremonial procedure, what about Him who was without spot and blemish?

Jesus, on the other hand, made no protest. He was condemned to die in our stead, and He accepted the judgment as if it were His very own. His own it was by willing substitution. He was led as a lamb to the slaughter, and the things to which Simon of Cyrene objected were even more odious to the spotless Son of God. He despised the shame, the unspeakable disgrace, but He went without the camp, bearing the reproach. While the cross bore heavily upon His weary body, the reproach pressed more weightily upon His blessed heart. The combined load, however, could not over-balance the weight of love He had for our poor, helpless, hopeless souls. Greater love hath no one than this. Instead of honour, it was dishonour; instead of reverence, it was cursing; instead of appreciation, it was deprecation; instead of reception, it was rejection; instead of a throne, it was a cross.

It should be observed that the position of our Lord is always central. From the Tree of Life in the Garden of Eden to the Lamb upon the Throne of Glory, the positional emphasis is invariably "in the midst". He promised to be in the midst of those who gather in His name. John saw Him in the midst of the lampstands in his apocalyptic vision. Even in death there was no exception, for on either side was one and Jesus in the middle. There, silhouetted not only against horizon's sill, but against history's ineffaceable outline, "He was numbered with the transgressors."

Jesus was ever cognizant of the end to which He would come. He thus informed His disciples. We come upon Him as one day He "began to teach them".[1] This was a school of theology indeed. The outline of His lesson on this occasion can be listed tersely as follows:

1. The Son of man *must* suffer.
2. The Son of man *must* be rejected.
3. The Son of man *must* be killed.
4. The Son of man *must* be raised.

A Place of Disrepute

The place of execution was always *extra portam, post urbem*—outside the gate, beyond the city. "Wherefore Jesus also, that he might sanctify the people with His own blood, suffered without the gate."[2] Golgotha was synonymous with criminals. It marked the *poena maxima*—the severest penalty of Jewish jurisprudence. Thus the place was held in disrepute. It was colloquially common in Bible times to say, "Can any good thing come out of Nazareth?" It was equally axiomatic to cry, "Golgotha for the good-for-nothings". It should affect us noticeably that, because of our sins, such a hideous experience befell the blessed Son of God. For "they led Him away."[3] Nor was it an organized march. It was characterized by excited enmity. It was a disgracefully memorable parade. Those who walked this "last mile" were treated with disdain and inhuman abuse.

"And he bearing his cross went forth into a place called the place of a skull."[4] He went; He went to a place; He went to a place of shame; He went bearing His cross. And never forget it, He went in our stead. It is a momentous thing that the Lord of Glory should thus be humbled. Surely He made Himself of "no reputation".[5] The Egyptian bondage, the lions' den, the fiery furnace, the Philippian jail, the Isle of Patmos—what were these in comparison with the Place of the Skull when it came to unmitigated dis-

[1]Mark 8: 31   [2]Heb. 13: 12   [3]Jno. 19: 16   [4]Jno. 19: 17   [5]Phil. 2: 7

grace? Is it to be wondered that the sun refused to shine? Is it surprising that the heavens groaned with thunderous reverberations? Is it to be thought strange that the breast of mother earth should tremble? The King eternal, God incarnate, was led by wicked men to a point of shameful indignity and in the company of condemned criminals. For this reason, and for this reason alone, we might object to the translators of Luke giving the place such a sweet-sounding name as *Calvary*. "Golgotha" is a trifle harder, while "skull" seems most appropriate. It was a place of disrepute.

The Place of Derision

"And they that passed by reviled him, wagging their heads."[6] This verse has given rise to the prevailing impression of commentators that the crucifixion took place beside a public highway. Surely this thought is not implied. Was this the conduct of quiet sojourners who chanced to pass at this particular time? Unthinkable! This is the display of those who cried for His death and hounded Him to this place of execution. Their evil hearts in diabolical excitement are now reaching the ultimate of vitriolic and vile outbursts as they march back and forth before the impaled Creator. From the very time it was said, "There was no room for them in the inn,"[7] until this present moment, it has been most evident that this world has had no desire for the Saviour. But, let us witness more closely the verse at hand.

"THEY" — THE DESIGNATION OF CHRIST REJECTORS. In Noah's time, before the judgment of God fell, *"They"* were eating and drinking, marrying and giving in marriage. When Abraham interceded with heart-stirring prayers for the people of Sodom, pleading that God would spare the city if he could find ten righteous men there, *"They"* said, "Stand back".[8] In Elijah's time, *"They"* said, "O Baal, hear us!"[9] In Matthew's record of the crucifixion, not less than ten times do we find the word *"They"* as designating those who violently rejected the Christ of God.

---

[6]Matt. 27: 39   [7]Luke 2: 7   [8]Gen. 19: 9   [9]1 Kings 18: 26

"Passed By" — The Most Unpardonable of All Their
Acts. They were passing by the only door to heaven,
for it was He who said, "I am the door; by me if any man
enter in, he shall be saved."[10] They were passing by the
only Saviour, for "there is none other name under heaven
given among men, whereby we must be saved."[11] They
were passing to their doom. It seems superfluous to sing,
"Pass me not, O gentle Saviour, hear my humble cry;
while on others Thou art calling, do not pass me by." More
accurately, it is not the Saviour who is passing by men; it
is men passing by the Saviour. Even though the sinners
at the cross taunted Him, jeered, mocked, smote, pierced
and maltreated Him in a multiplicity of manners, paradise
would have been their prospect—indeed, their realization,
if only they had joined with the one malefactor, saying,
"Lord, remember me". But they passed by!

"Reviled"— The Offensive Odour of Their Corrupt
Nature. The vociferous taunts which were hurled at
the dying Saviour in these moments of His intense agony
were the results of mob psychology. It is likely that one
originated the words while others joined their voices in
a concerted railing, filling the whole countryside with
their boisterous denunciation of the spotless Lamb of God.
"Thou that destroyest the temple and buildest it in three
days, save thyself,"[12] they shouted with wicked glee. "If
thou be the Son of God, come down from the cross." It is
unmistakably clear that this was the *Father of Lies*[13] moti-
vating his children in an attempt to disprove the truth of
Jesus' statements. As he once brought Samson into the
temple of Dagon to "make sport" for the three thousand
hissing, depraved people who looked on, even so he seeks
now to put our Lord to shame in this solemn hour. Yes,
Golgotha was the place of derision.

"Wagging Their Heads" — A Gesture of Rejection.
It would seem that their wicked emotions had been whipped
into such fitful intensity that gestures must be added to
their expressed animosity for the sake of emphasis. Per-

[10]Jno. 10: 9   [11]Acts 4: 12   [12]Matt. 27: 40   [13]Jno. 8: 44

haps the superscription above the head of Jesus had caused this. Pilate had written, over the persecutors' protest, *"This is Jesus the King of the Jews".*[14]

As the nodding of the head is a positive gesture, betokening agreement or acceptance, so the wagging of the head is a negative motion, indicating disagreement or rejection. When they saw the word "JESUS", which means Saviour, they wagged their heads violently. He was *not* their saviour. When they saw the words "KING OF THE JEWS" they wagged their heads in firm denial. He was *not* their king. They had no king but Caesar. One hundred and five thousand passed by the bier of Babe Ruth, of baseball fame, to pay their respects. This uncounted number passed by the cross of Christ to show their disrespect. Actions speak louder than words. Golgotha was the place of derision.

A Place of Death

"There they crucified him."[15] This is precisely why they placed a cross upon the Lord and paraded Him to this particular point. Since every other detail developed with prophetic exactness, is it not reasonable to assume that the Place of the Skull was minutely marked out in the blueprints of Omniscience? This was true of His birth: "But thou, Bethlehem Ephratah, though thou be little among the thousands of Judah, yet out of thee shall he come forth unto me that is to be ruler in Israel."[16] Concerning His second advent, it is stated, "His feet shall stand in that day upon the mount of Olives, which is before Jerusalem on the east."[17] The point of His decease was just as specifically planned, and Calvary was the place.

This bald, bleak, skull-like mound reeked with the very atmosphere of death. It did not need to have skeletons strewn around, as some suppose, in order to give it the ghastly cast of a life-destroying scene. It was commonly known as the place of death. People referred to Golgotha as the residents of New York State refer to Sing Sing. A

---

[14]Matt. 27: 37   [15]Jno. 19: 18   [16]Micah 5: 2   [17]Zech. 14: 4

judge, in rendering his verdict, did not necessarily employ the word "crucifixion". It would have been, and perhaps was, sufficient merely to say, "Golgotha". That meant doom.

It seems incredible that the Mighty Maker should be fitted into such an ignominious picture—the Creator of the Creation crucified! The explanation, of course, is that God "hath made him to be sin (the sin-offering) for us".[18] The verdict against us was death. As our substitute, He died for us—at the place of execution. Golgotha was *that* place.

The Place of Pondering

"But Peter followed him afar off unto the high priest's palace, and went in, and sat with the servants, to see the end"—Matthew 26:58.

HEN JESUS WAS BROUGHT before Caiaphas the high priest, Peter, together with the servants of the palace, sat down "to see the end". What end did they expect to see? The end of His teaching? The end of His ministry? The end of His following? The end of Christ Himself? We cannot be too sure what was in the minds of Peter and his ill-gotten associates as they watched and waited. It was not patient passivity, but the delusion of an impossible neutrality. They were merely sitting on the sidelines— simply spectators from the galleries. But there is no neutral position when it comes to Christ and His death. One is either for Him or against Him.

Paradoxical as it may appear, the end to which Christ was then coming, the end for which He was born, was an end, the end of which shall never be seen. They were watching Him who is Himself THE END even as He is the beginning. The Cross was not the end of Christ's teaching. His teaching continues with all the freshness, beauty and force which it possessed when it fell from those blessed lips which spake as never man spake. That it might continue, the resurrected Christ met with His disciples just prior to His glorious ascension and outlined the directions for a continuation of that which He "began both to do and teach".[1]

Nor was the Cross the end of His ministry, for the blessings of His Word, the power of His grace, the wisdom of His counsel and the sweetness of His comfort still reach un-

[1]Acts 1: 1, 2

23

told hearts in the most remote parts of the earth. And the Cross did not end His following. People of every tribe and nation have bowed humbly at His blessed feet in faithful acceptance of salvation and have earnestly contended for the faith, some even going to prisons and the burning stakes. Today, as never before, His servants push forward to the ends of the earth as faithful ambassadors, personal representatives of the King of kings. Neither was the Cross the end of Christ, for, after plunging into the river of death, He emerged on the resurrection side with the victory shout: "Because I live, ye shall live also."[2] To John on the Isle of Patmos, He said "I am he that liveth, and was dead: and, behold, I am alive for evermore."[3] His work is just as eternal as Himself. His is an eternal purpose. His ministry must continue, else we are of all men most miserable. It will continue, "for the Lord of hosts hath purposed, and who shall turn it back?"[4] Yet the spectators sat down to see the end.

There is a sense in which the Cross may be pondered with profit. By the term, *the Cross*, we mean, not the physical instrument of death, but the work which was so gloriously accomplished thereon.

The Malefactor Pondered the Cross

Yes, the dying thief rejoiced to see that Fountain in his day. And he will never cease to rejoice. The second malefactor was just as near to the Fountain, and though thirsty, refused to drink. This is the travesty of human indifference. Some believe; others discredit. Some receive; others reject.

HE REVERED GOD. This man who found a place in the *Who's Who* of Sacred Writ had to look beyond the centre cross to see the third. He must have gazed upon the Saviour as he spoke. "Dost thou not fear God?"[5] He demanded. His question was, by inference, his own positive testimony. As he pondered the Cross, the first thing which occurred to his mind in his intense anguish was the fear of God. This is the beginning of wisdom,[6] for "a prudent man

[2]Jno. 14: 19 [3]Rev. 1: 18 [4]Isa. 14: 27 [5]Luke 23: 40 [6]Prov. 9: 10

foreseeth the evil (judgment), and hideth himself; but the simple pass on, and are punished."[7]

HE RENOUNCED SELF. The malefactor confessed his guilt, approved the court's verdict and recognized his doom. "We receive the due reward of our deeds,"[8] he lamented. He had not a single commendation concerning himself. His attitude was, "Nothing in my hand I bring, simply to Thy Cross I cling." He was in no condition to die, but in the right condition to believe. He was at the end of self. He sensed his worthlessness and knew his helplessness. Whether or not men sin against the State, as did this man, all have sinned against God, and none is any more worthy of salvation than was he. His pride was dissipated; his purpose was definite; his profession was clear. This put the dying thief in the very centre of the best position in which to receive the gift of life through the Saviour.

HE RESPECTED CHRIST. "This man hath done nothing amiss," he reasoned, while pain was piercing his being. Apart from Pilate's wife, he was the only human defence witness willing to speak in behalf of the innocence of Jesus. Where was boastful Peter? Where was the beloved disciple? Where are the sunshine testimonies when the storms are raging? Where is the Church of Christ in this crucial hour? Perhaps in the palace of pleasure, just sitting and waiting for the *end*. Prophetically, we are told that Jesus looked for comforters, but found none.[9] Does this prophecy conflict with the malefactor's statement? No. This was not sympathy. This was a statement of appraisal on the part of a stranger. It was nevertheless an evidence of respect.

HE REQUESTED SALVATION. Since divine salvation is a gift, one does not need to ask for it. One simply takes it by faith and receives it with appreciation. But witness two facts: *First*, this was before the "veil of the temple was rent in the midst".[10] It was yet in that period when sincere, repentant people cried, "God be merciful to

[7]Prov. 22: 3   [8]Luke 23: 40, 41 [9]Psa. 69: 20   [10]Luke 23: 45

me, a sinner!"[11] *Second,* it is not so much the statement of the lips as it is the state of the heart which counts. Some, when passing from death to life, kneel while others stand; some weep while others smile; some are calm while others are noticeably moved, yet all are soundly saved if they trust in the Lord Jesus Christ. The malefactor said, "Lord, remember me when thou comest into thy kingdom".[12] He confessed Jesus as Lord and believed in his heart the fact of resurrection. Though Jesus were dying, he believed He would come into His kingdom. Such believing brings salvation.

The Roman Centurion Pondered the Cross

HE WAS ALERT. We observe that the centurion was "watching Jesus".[14] It is evident that the eyes of all were focussed upon the Saviour. He was the central figure. He is always the prominent personality. The centurion was alert in the performance of his duty. He was there to guard the three crosses, but his eyes were fastened upon the middle one.

HE WAS ALARMED. To stand guard at crucifixions while on occupational duty for Rome was not a new experience for this veteran soldier. At this particular time, however, there was a difference—a tremendous difference, singular developments. The sun went into mourning with a three-hour blackout; the heavens moaned with thunderous groans, while the breast of mother earth trembled until the rocks began to crack and the graves began to open. Soldiers who have been through fiery ordeals are not too easily frightened, but the centurion and his company "feared greatly". But, must God shake the earth to stir the hearts of men to an acknowledgment of His son?

HE WAS ACCURATE. "Truly, this was the Son of God,"[15] he firmly avowed. He was right in his appraisal but wrong in his timing. Note the tense of the verb. The Great White Throne judgment scene has been dramatically depicted by poet, penman and preacher, but none has ever been

---

[11]Luke 18: 13   [12]Lu. 23: 42   [18]Rom. 10: 9   [14]Matt. 27: 54   [15]Ibid

able to fully assay the deep, deathly disillusionment of those who there discover that it *was* the Son of God they had dishonoured, disbelieved, rejected. How eminently essential is it for eyes to be opened *now* to that which God Himself avows is true.

The Apostle Peter Pondered the Cross

He saw the prophets' hope fulfilled. However nebulous may have been Peter's former outlook, however unsteady his heart, he is now a man with a new vision and an unswerving poise. He was a competent eyewitness of what the prophets looked for but the fulfilment of which they did not see. "Of which salvation," he tells us, "the prophets have inquired and searched diligently, who prophesied of the grace that should come, searching what, or what manner of time the Spirit of Christ which was in them did signify, when it testified beforehand the sufferings of Christ."[16] Even though Peter was, at the time, a vacillating disciple, following afar off and sitting in the enemy camp to warm his hands, he nevertheless saw what the prophets died without seeing.

He saw the preciousness of the blood of Christ. Peter, with Paul, was very clear on the basic essentials of the faith. If one is wrong on the meaning of the Cross, one is wrong on every important matter concerning Christ. If you were to ask the beloved Apostle how we are redeemed, there would be neither hesitancy nor equivocation. "With the precious blood of Christ, as of a lamb without blemish and without spot,"[17] would be his quick and faithful reply. And this is the value of the work of Christ on the Cross. He shed His blood for the remission of sin. The life is in the blood, thus He poured out His life for all mankind.

He saw the purpose of the crucifixion. The death of Christ was not for the purpose, primarily, of removing sins, as vital as that is. The people of God's hand had become estranged from Him. They had to be brought back. Jesus came to seek and to save the lost. He died to bring men to

[16] Pet. 1: 10, 11   [17] 1 Peter 1: 19

God. But how could sin-marred man come into contact with a holy God? Their sins had produced a separation.[18] There was a barrier. There must be removal before there can be reunion. Observe how clearly Peter saw this when he said, "For Christ also hath once suffered for sins, the just for the unjust that he might bring us to God, being put to death in the flesh, but quickened by the Spirit."[19] Thus, while there are between God and man distance, difference and deception, Calvary cares for it all.

The Apostle Paul Pondered the Cross

THE APOSTLE'S IDENTIFICATION WITH THE CROSS. Paul made a business of living the Christian life. It absorbed his thoughts, his time and his energy. So completely had he become a new creation, and so utterly had the former things disappeared from his life, that he could confidently assert, "I am crucified with Christ".[20] This is more factual than figurative. As stated elsewhere in this volume, he met hatred at its bitterest, rejection at its saddest, poverty at its depth, mockery at its worst, misunderstanding at its height, sorrow at its deepest, enmity at its fiercest, and death at its cruelest. But while it was an actual experience with Paul, it was more spiritual than physical. He reckoned the old Saul of Tarsus to have been nailed to the Cross—having died with Christ.

THE APOSTLE'S INTEREST IN THE CROSS. The interest of one crucified with Christ could lie only in that which had brought new-found joys, unprecedented opportunities and the prospect of glory. Paul witnessed the folk about him boasting in the precepts and ceremonies which had been done away in the sacrificial work of Calvary. "God forbid," he emphatically asserted, "that I should glory, save in the cross of our Lord Jesus Christ."[21] The Cross held an appeal for him which excelled and overpowered all else. It towered over the wrecks of time. He found it alone to be dross-refining, pride-consuming, spirit-lifting and faith-promoting.

---

[18]Isa. 59: 2   [19]1 Pet. 3: 18   [20]Gal. 2: 20   [21]Gal. 6: 14

THE APOSTLE'S INTENTION CONCERNING THE CROSS. As to the intention of Paul we need have no doubt. He was determined to know nothing save Jesus Christ and Him crucified.[22] His intention, indeed his determination, was to make available to others the message which had introduced him to such holy, happy privileges. It might have appeared foolish to many,[23] but he firmly pledged himself to a faithful proclamation of the Cross. It is the message alone which promises peace and prospect to a hopeless race. It is the only assurance of heaven. It has a transforming power, an enlightening force, and an encouraging strength. This is the Pauline view of the Cross of Christ.

The Father Pondered the Cross

"If we receive the witness of men," the Apostle John reminds us, "the witness of God is greater." Nor is the Father silent on this all-important matter. In the final analysis, God was the principle one to be satisfied. Was He?

THE SON REGARDED BY THE FATHER. Both at the baptism of Jesus and at His transfiguration, heaven bent low to broadcast the Father's approval. "This is my beloved Son in whom I am well pleased," said the voice from the most excellent Glory. There never was a moment when it was otherwise. Jesus was perfect in His walk, word, and work. The Father saw His conduct and heard His conversation. He watched Him executing the plans which they had laid conjointly in eternity past. He witnessed His justice being vindicated and observed His righteousness being protected. God was well pleased with Calvary's accomplishment.

THE SON WAS RAISED BY THE FATHER. We cannot move very far into such solemn considerations, but we know that it was the "God of peace that brought again from the dead our Lord Jesus Christ".[24] By the resurrection, Jesus was "declared the Son of God with power".[25] All of this proves conclusively the deep satisfaction of the Father as He viewed the work of the Cross.

---

[22]1 Cor. 2: 2   [23]1 Cor. 1: 18   [24]Heb. 13: 20   [25]Rom. 1: 4

THE SON WAS RECEIVED BY THE FATHER. We may know what it means to welcome home a son from a far-flung battle front where victory has been won, but we cannot now know what it was like for the Saviour to return to the Father's right hand. The Holy Spirit, through Paul, simply explained that He was "received up into glory".[26] Yes, the Father pondered the Cross. He saw all that transpired, even within the enshrouding darkness. His acceptance of the work of Christ is proved in that He regarded His Son with the fullest of pleasure, raised Him with the greatest of power and received Him with the richest of honour.

If Calvary can stand infinite scrutiny, let us be assured that the message of the Cross which we preach can withstand the most caustic criticism of the skeptic, atheist and infidel. Let us, likewise, glory only in the Cross of our Lord Jesus Christ.

---

[26]1 Tim. 3: 16

The Place of Pressure

"Who for the joy that was set before him endured the cross, despising the shame."— Hebrews 12:2.

Devotion may, with reverent carefulness, step behind the scene of Calvary. Within the enshrouding darkness, the lamp of prophecy brings to light what otherwise would remain obscured from even the most discerning student. For, if the rigours of the Cross were indescribably severe, then also was its reproach unspeakably sorrowful.

The weight of the Cross was the way to the crown. One must be clear concerning His death before one can properly consider His resurrection and future glory. Apart from His suffering and shame there would be no salvation. Jesus told the disciples that he would suffer many things. He may have delineated the kinds of mistreatment which wicked hands would inflict upon Him. He may not have done so. In any event, He did reveal sufficient to stir the heart of Peter, for Peter "began to rebuke Him."

Let us not misunderstand either Peter's manner or his method. It was not an attempted correction of what he thought to be a mistaken comment on the part of his Lord. It was, rather, a violent objection to the very idea that such experiences should befall one so lovely as Christ. It was the reaction which true affection would exhibit at any time if a threat were made to harm one so loved. Then Jesus began to enlighten Peter on this point. What Jesus said to him must be taken in its entirety to be properly understood. Peter was simply looking at it from the human point of view. We have no doubt that Satan was working in many subtle ways to frustrate our Saviour's expiatory work, even through this disciple, but the fact remains that the thought of His Lord being put to shame was most

31

disconcerting to the Apostle. As yet, he knew not the truth
concerning Jesus' sufferings.

The Revealed Embarrassment

We shall see His lovely face some bright golden morning. Until then, we shall not know how tender and how
sweet His countenance is. We are prone, and it becomes
pleasant enjoyment, to make our own deductions and to
establish our own impressions. Every artist depicts a
graciousness of His facial expression, while poets write
about the kindliness of His countenance. One who so
readily attracted little children could not have had a stern
appearance, nor could one who comforted and counselled
have presented the features of austerity.

We witness the Lord Jesus as He looked upon the sorrowing family of Bethany. We observe Him as He gazed upon
hopeless lepers in the odiousness of their dread disease. We
see Him as He turned His eyes toward the weeping widow
of Nain. We watch Him as He evidenced joy in the exceptional faith of the Centurion whose servant was sick unto
death. We note His upturned face to summon Zacchaeus
from the sycamore tree. We are solemnly impressed as, with
pure affection, He turns toward His beloved disciple in
tender solicitude, telling him to comfort His mother. No
ordinary countenance this. It mirrored the glory of God
and revealed the love of His heart.

Now, in the wretched hour of Golgotha's most horrible
execution, a surge from the soul of the Saviour leaps the
bounds of inaudibility and overflows His blessed lips.
"Shame hath covered my face,"[2] His heart wearily cried.
His words were tinged with saddened innocence. It was
hardly an announcement to the spectators. And it was by
no means an apology. It was rather a whispered heartache.
Nor was He referring only or specifically to the plucking of
His beard by evil hands which left His visage so marred
that He did not resemble a man.[3] No, it was the consum-
mate weight of all the disgraceful things which had been
meted out to Him. He felt that the embarrassment of His

---

[2]Psa. 69: 7   [3]Isa. 52: 14

soul was being registered in His face, for the countenance betrays the emotions. How shall we ever begin to survey the magnitude of His sacrificial experience!

The Crushing Impact of Shame

"The reproaches of them that reproached thee are fallen upon me,"[4] the Saviour prophetically whispered to the Father in the midst of His sorrow. Note the word *fallen*. There was not a gradual imposition of maltreatment going successively from one stage to another with a slight increase of intensity in the development. Rather did it seem that all hell had pounced upon God's humble Lamb with sudden and sustained violence with no surcease until sin's lashing storm had spent its force utterly. The serpent's venom was poured upon our voluntary Sacrifice until He had absorbed it all.

It was as a falling weight. An adult can support a dead weight of twenty-five pounds on almost any part of his body with no evident discomfort for the time, but a one-pound solid dropped from above could produce excruciating pain and do far-reaching injury. The reproaches *fell* upon the Saviour. They were sins against the Father. All sin is essentially and foremostly against God. "Against thee, and thee only have I sinned," David lamented. Jesus, in dying for the sins of the world, bore these reproaches.

The Subject of Base Ridicule

There is nothing that would more quickly keep most people in seclusion than to know they were the object of ridicule by the public at large. Yet this is precisely the kind of shame Jesus innocently suffered. "They that sit in the gate speak against me,"[5] He revealed.

Who were they that sat in the gate? In modern times, it is difficult to visualize certain ancient customs. The gate of a walled city was the point of entrance and exit. Thus, the populace was funnelled into this narrow channel. It was the ideal point at which to air one's views, to publicize one's wares and to solicit attention for any given

---

[4]Psa. 69: 9   [5]Psa. 69: 12a

purpose. It became the favourite place for boulevard phil-
osophers, vocal critics and idle gossipers. Jesus knew He
would be the topic of discussion—the news highlight of the
year—among the crowds at the gate. He would be spoken
of as a perverter of the people; a self-designated religious
leader who sought to supplant Judaism but was cut short;
a distorter of facts in His claim to be God; a criminal properly punished.

Then, too, knowing the end from the beginning, He saw
full well the gay scenes of human debauchery where His
holy name was trampled in wicked mirth. "I was the song
of the drunkards,"[6] He sadly commented. Perhaps no sinfulness is so pathetic as that which is perpetrated when
intoxication has robbed one of all moral restraint. We have
at some time witnessed public spectacles of shamefulness,
but how wild and weird must be the orgies where wickedness is unleashed to the limit by perverted hearts and in-
toxicated minds. Think of our dear, precious Saviour in all
His holiness becoming the theme of songs from such lips.
Imagine vice dens, reeking with the very atmosphere of
hell, being filled with parodies on hymns to blaspheme the
Lord of glory. Little wonder His face was covered with
shame. Little wonder His soul was weighted with sorrow.

The Sad Spectacle in Full View of the Father

"Thou hast known my reproach, and my shame, and
my dishonour; mine adversaries are all before thee,"[7] the
Saviour sadly recounted. This was another whispered
prayer, prophetically presented, which we do not hear amid
the thunders of Calvary.

It was sad enough for the stoical faces of chief priests
in decadent Judaism to be looking on while He was tortured
in body and soul, but sadder to Him by far was the fact that
His Father in Heaven could see it all. If the heart of one
is right, and a shameful experience befalls that one, it is
ever and always the desire, above all else, that those near
and dear shall not know about it. As a pastor, it has been
our experience many times to counsel with those who have

6Psa. 69: 12b   7Psa. 69: 19

fallen into deep disgrace, at which times we have heard the question tearfully put, "You won't let mother know about it, will you?" Or perhaps it is a father, a wife, a husband from whom such knowledge is desired to be kept.

This is a feeble illustration and falls far short of usefulness, but perhaps our solemn hearts and reverent minds can begin to see how much the Lord Jesus, being spit upon, smitten, mocked and scorned, would have the pains in His heart deepened because His Father knew it all—His reproach, His shame, His dishonour. The Father saw His adversaries as well—Judas in His treachery, the marauding horde that bound and led Him, the coldness and indifference of Annas and Caiaphas, the vacillating weakness of Pilate, the rushing, ridiculing throng en route to Golgotha, the drivers of the nails and the wagging heads of the cynical.

The Irony of Bitterness

"They gave me also gall for my meat; and in my thirst they gave me vinegar to drink,"[8] the Saviour added. Perhaps the multiplied bitternesses, by contrast, made His love seem sweeter and His work more wonderful. When He was hungry, they gave Him gall; when thirsty, vinegar. He could have changed the gall into the sweetest of honey and the vinegar into the nectar of fresh wine. But He did not. He must needs suffer. He could have changed the stones into bread in the wilderness, even as Satan suggested. But He did not. He must needs be tested as was the first Adam. He could have flown when He was tired instead of trekking in the sand to meet the needy soul at Jacob's well. But He did not. "He *must* needs go through Samaria." He Who could have played with the stars as a little boy plays with marbles, could have changed the Cross into a throne. But he did not. He Who commanded the hosts of heaven could have ordered even His persecutors to do His bidding. But He did not. *He must needs suffer many things.* This was part of the shame. The gall and the vinegar but reminded of the bitterness of sinful hearts and the greatness of human need.

[8] Psa. 69: 21

The Saviour Deserted in His Deepest Grief

"I loked for some to take pity, but there was none,"[9] He solemnly revealed. He whose eyes run to and fro upon the earth scanned the crowd about the Cross to see if there were just one tear of sympathy, only to have His anguish deepened that none was to be found. Perhaps we are justified in believing that this was the humanity of Jesus in its tender display. Who would not have felt likewise? Even God Himself wants to be remembered. Nobody desires to be forgotten, not even in death.

> *"Don't, don't forget Jesus.*
> *So loving, so tender, so true;*
> *When you were in darkness and sin,*
> *Jesus remembered you."*

But this is not the full expression of His heavy heart. He further stated, "I looked . . . for comforters, but I found none."[10] How wonderful had it been if some one, even one, had pushed through the spear-armed guards at the risk of his life and had fallen to his knees before the Cross; then, with upturned, pitying eyes had called out with tearful appreciation, "Lord Jesus, it is of thy mercies we are not all consumed. Thy compassions fail not. Thou art, in Thy great and boundless love, dying for me who am a wretched, hopeless sinner." And then to have added, before a spear pierced him through, "Lord Jesus, I love Thee for dying in my place." But none did—not even one. Alone He bore the pressure, which, according to Webster, is a painful bodily or mental feeling as of a weight or burden.

There were so many factors surrounding the Cross that the mind of man staggers before the divine revelation, and the intellect, however keen, must confess inability of comprehension. But this we know, the heart of Christ was lacerated noticeably. We may not be able to prove that He died OF a broken heart, but we are sure that He died WITH a broken heart. His own testimony settles the point: "Reproach hath broken my heart."[11]

---

[9]Psa. 69: 20b   [10]Psa. 69: 20c   [11]Psa. 69: 20

The Place of Pain

"For Christ also hath once suffered for sins"
—I Pet., 3:18.

Nowhere, we are led to believe, do the rays of divine light beam with more brilliance than in their focus upon the Cross of Calvary. In these rays, we discover a series of antitheses, but they harmonize with the divine purpose as the various colours and hues blend into the amazing beauty of the rainbow—wrath and love, pain and pleasure, judgment and innocence, malice and justice, blasphemy and forgiveness, mockery and mirth, cursing and blessing.

What towering truth inheres in the redemptive program. Its message is the basis of all orthodox belief and the bulwark of the whole Christian structure. Each segment of its proclamation is a satisfying proof of accurate scriptural prediction and a justifying support for all the confidence of which man is capable. In simple and unequivocal language, as forceful as it is simple, the dear old Gospel story is sweetly presented as a matter of transcendent import and is absolutely incontrovertible, irrefutable and inimitable. It can withstand, as it has withstood, every polemic attack, every satanic rebuttal, every vicious intent of the skeptic, agnostic and infidel. Still it stands gloriously, firmer than the rock of Gibraltar, glistening in the beauty and brilliance of its own inherent divine qualities.

In the blueprints of Omniscience, ere the world took shape, the specifications of the world's rescue and wonderful Rescuer were minutely traced. They were clearly destined to be transmuted into a satisfying reality. They present the fact of the crucifixion, the acts of the crucifiers and the feelings of the Crucified. Every step in the develop-

ment is intensely significant. The artist has exhausted his
skill in attempting a vivid portrayal, while the poet, penman and preacher find therein new food for thought and
more material for messages as the ages unfold. Not only
this, but every humble son of Adam who has had this
glorious truth impressed upon his mind and written in
his heart never ceases to marvel at the mountainous love
it all bespeaks. Unfurl the banner of the Cross; and wher-
ever it floats in this world of conspicuous bitterness and
conflicting emphases, it invariably spells H-O-P-E for all
people everywhere. Love's language is never misunder-
stood. It may be rejected, but it always presents its message.

When we gird up the loins of our minds and linger
at Calvary we cannot but become conscious of the infinite
cost of our wonderful salvation. In this meditation, we
face several pertinent facts, namely, the reasonableness,
the rigours, and the rescue of the Cross.

The Reasonableness of the Cross

To refer to the Cross as reasonable, meets with an immediate inward objection. It conflicts with our imperfect
impressions. Of course, His thoughts are higher than our
thoughts, and His ways are not our ways. If the Cross with
all its ignominy was the cost of our redemption, and if Jesus
came to pay the ransom price, then is it not reasonable that
He should be impaled? There could not have been a negoti-
ated peace; therefore, there could not have been a com-
promised price. What the law demanded, He was willing,
and even more than willing, to meet. The exactions may
have been unreasonable, but it is not unreasonable that He
would submit to them all.

The ultimatum, divinely given, required the death penalty for sin. If Jesus Christ was sinful man's substitute,
and He was, is it not reasonable that He should have died
in man's place. If the substitutionary process necessitated
His being made a curse for us, and if the hanging on a tree
constituted a curse, is it not reasonable that He should
have been lifted up so ingloriously? That is, it is reasonable

that the blessed Son of God would do all that was needed, all that was demanded, all that was designed for our ultimate deliverance from the throes and thraldom of sin. What a Saviour!

The Rigours of the Cross

The rigours of the Cross cannot be so tersely treated. Neither can they be so adequately defined. Whether our Lord was forced to carry only the crossbeam (the patibulum) or the complete instrument of death, including the crossbeam the upright (the palus), is hardly a point for debate. We are told that He staggered under the load. That is enough. And whether His blessed body was nailed to the instrument of death before it was dropped with a sudden thud into the excavated provision, or whether He was hoisted to the crossbeam after the tree was planted, is equally not a point for empty speculation. The Word tells us specifically that He suffered. That, too, is enough. The dramatic is decidedly irrelevant in the portrayal of this solemn and significant event. Orr's encyclopedia asserts that "one who dies by crucifixion dies not one but a thousand deaths." The pain was excruciating and the agony indescribable. His beard was plucked; His body was bent; His head was bruised; His side was pierced; His heart was broken. How can anyone question the great love with which He loved us?

The rigours of the Cross exacted their toll mentally as well as physically. Yet, in the throes of this cruel world's brutal treatment, He could ask forgiveness for the inflictors of the pain which He endured. He could look with incomparable love upon those who added to the shame He so much despised. There He was tempted by satan, forsaken by God, deserted by friends and plagued by the imps of hell. All the while, the "bulls of Bashan" stampeded in their mockery and invective railing at the base of the Cross. Then, the curtain of darkness was drawn as the fulness and fierceness of divine wrath was visited upon Him. What transpired under that shroud of thick darkness is known only to Him Whose counsels are wise and Whose doings are wonderful in our eyes. This, we assuredly know, "He was wounded for our transgressions and bruised for our iniquities."

The Rescue of the Cross

If the rigours of the Cross defy adequate description, what shall we say concerning its rescue? We must at once become beggars for words, for the values of Calvary are inestimable. The far-reaching effects are inconceivable. The Cross is the Life-line to a perishing humanity. The Cross bridged the chasm between the Almighty Creator and His alienated creatures. It is the dividing point between life and death, between hope and despair, between heaven and hell. Through the Cross, we have sweet peace and complete pardon, joyful prospects and eternal provisions. When we are told that He ONCE died for sins, we know immediately that there was sufficiency and satisfaction as well as severity in His accomplishment.

> "He breaks the pow'r of cancelled sin,
>   He sets the prisoner free;
> His blood can make the foulest clean,
>   His blood availed for me."

Is there any question at all in our minds as to the willingness of the cultured Apostle Paul to prefer the Cross to the classics, to limit his message to the subject of Christ and His death? "For I determined to know nothing among you," he asserted, "save Jesus Christ and him crucified."[1] Yet, we watch the mental antics of some liberalistic theologians, and our whole being is aroused to an indignant pity that useful lives should be thus squandered. Pedantry, you know, is not merely an ostentatious display of learning, but often it is knowledge divorced from service and true devotion. Many, who feel a sense of intellectual superiority, delight in leading an earnest, humble soul-winner into a "modern Areopagus, there to sacrifice him by ridicule as gladiators were butchered to make a Roman holiday."

---

[1] 1 Cor. 2: 2

There are those in our day, however, be their number ever so small, who have appropriated the values of Calvary, who know the experience which salvation brings, who have unshatterable assurance, and rest in a steadfast hope. These are moved with deep compassion to direct others to the Lamb of God Who taketh away the sins of the world. A soul-winning effort in itself is convincing proof of one's own rescue through Christ's deliverance, for no one can very effectively proffer assistance and beckon cheer to those engulfed in the waves of sin if that one, himself, were not established on the shore of resurrection ground.

But the rescue! How solemn, and yet how elevated are our thoughts as we ponder the matter. It is the rescue of a race we have in mind—the human race—a race that had lost its oneness with the thrice-holy God, a race that had forfeited its right to live. Visualize, if you can, the deluded parents of our human family being rejected from the Garden of Eden. Note their disillusionment and despair. See the heavenly sentinels rushing to guard the entrance, flashing their flaming swords with greater aptitude than an expert drum major wielding a baton. Then and there began to flow the swelling stream of life's vicissitudes, varied and inevitable—experiences too common, too sorrowful, and too numerous to recount. Surely, "man is born unto trouble as the sparks fly upward."[2]

It was then that the obituary made its debut: "And all the days that Adam lived were nine hundred, thirty years, AND HE DIED . . . and all the years of Seth were nine hundred, twelve years, AND HE DIED . . . and all the days of Enos were nine hundred, five years, AND HE DIED." This terse clause, established through oft repetition in Genesis, has punctuated every biography down through the ages, with Enoch and Elijah only being excepted by divine interposition.

The Herculean task of the world's Creator was to curb the raging current of death which was flowing down, down —down the declivities of time toward the fearful falls which plunge men irretrievably into the lake of fire. But,

[2] Job 5: 7

"That He should leave His place on high,
And come for sinful man to die,
You count it strange? So once did I
Before I knew my Saviour."

We must carefully guard against distorting the colours of Calvary's scene. They, for the most part, are drab and unsightly; yet, even as the lightning dissipates for the moment the inky darkness of the midnight storm, just so, love and hope shine forth in overpowering brightness amid the gruesomeness of Golgotha. Jesus dealt with the enemy, wrestled with death, grappled with hell and emerged as the mighty conqueror.

"Look ye saints, the sight is glorious!
See the Man of Sorrows now;
From the fight returned victorious—
Every knee to Him shall bow."

When Jesus died for the sins of the world, He not only descended into Hades, but he ascended into Paradise, leading captivity captive, and giving deliverance to all those who had reposed faith in the coming Messiah-Emancipator. Yes, He broke the power of cancelled sin; He set the prisoner free. Today, the door of Grace stands widely ajar, and whosoever will may enter and be saved. Christ died for our sins according to the Scriptures, and we rest in the glad assurance of rescue from this body of death. We may exult in the promise, "Because I live, ye shall live also." This is victory at inestimable cost! This is a living, stimulating hope that penetrates the gloom of time and anchors the soul of the true believer in the brightness of glory.

The Place of Perplexity

"I find in him no fault, but ye have a custom"
John 18:38, 39.

FROM THE ANTEROOM OF GRIEF in the Garden of Gethsemane to the final paroxysm of anguish on the cruel Cross, each step was fraught with such unapproachable solemnity that human thought cannot follow too clearly the successive developments. We have a faint appreciation of the betrayal and the arrest, the appearance before Annas, the denial by Peter, the delivery to Caiaphas, the humiliation before Pilate, and the Saviour's release to the unprincipled multitude.

The whole of our Lord's bitter experience, as the shadows of ignominy began to lengthen, was an almost interminable succession of paradoxes. He who came to unbind was bound. He who came to lead was led. And when they reached the Gentile judgment hall, the Jews would not enter in lest they be defiled in the presence of the Holy One. This proves apparent incompatibility, but how sorely misjudged! He was wrong; they were right. He was wicked; they were righteous. He deserved death; it was their right to live. He was guilty; they were innocent. Such was the display of their wickedly warped attitude.

It was the time of the Passover. Their most prominent feast day was approaching, but they failed to comprehend that the One whom they were disgracing was the True Passover. Nor have the Jews had a paschal lamb acceptable to Jehovah since the rejection of Christ. None but a depraved mind would expect these rioting hearts of clamoring people to be in a suitable state to worship the Lord in the hours just before them.

Perhaps nowhere does the prophecy of Isaiah find a more appropriate application than just here. "To what purpose is the multitude of your sacrifices unto me?" "Bring no more vain obligations; incense is an abomination unto me; the new moons and the sabbaths, the calling of assemblies, I cannot away with; it is iniquity, even the solemn meeting (day of atonement). And when ye spread forth your hands, I will hide mine eyes from you; yea, when ye make many prayers, I will not hear; your hands are full of blood."[1]

The Matter Summarized

THE PERSISTENCE OF THE PEOPLE.[2] The chief contention of the people who brought Jesus to the Roman court—the evil desire of their wicked hearts—was that Jesus should die. This fact was made crystal clear. Nothing short of such a verdict would quell their rioting emotions. They could not, by virtue of their own legal restrictions, exact His life. Therefore, they brought pressure to bear upon the Roman judge in order that he might grant them their desire through his good offices. The gracious, tender, loving Son of God was totally unacceptable to their blinded hearts. It has ever been so. It is so today. No one can give a logical, properly-founded reason for the pronounced heart aversion toward Christ, yet few people find room for Jesus. He is not wanted.

THE PERPLEXITY OF PILATE.[3] Pilate's problems were prominent. He lacked utterly the poise of a judge. His statements were not carefully weighed. His words were noticeably incoherent. His mien and method lacked the dignity such an office boasts. He found himself in a difficult plight. Before him stood the personification of Wisdom, but his questions went unanswered. Before him stood the world's great Comforter, but his mind remained unsettled. Before him stood the Wonderful Counsellor, but his problems were unsolved. Before him stood the only

[1]Isa. 1: 11, 12, 15 [2]Jno. 18: 23-32 [3]Jno. 18: 33-38

Saviour, but his soul was unsaved. The most tactful thing of which Pilate's mind was capable, he expressed in these words, "But ye have a custom."[4] Why did he not say with strong conviction, "The Roman law reads thus and so?" Or, why did he not preserve the honour of his position by stating, "Justice demands fairness; verdicts are rendered only on the strength of the evidence presented?" Thus, while Jesus died by the predeterminate counsel of God,[5] He was killed by the custom of men.

THE PURPOSE OF PROVIDENCE. Perhaps the loneliness of the Saviour in the judgment hall has entirely escaped our notice heretofore. The Jewish populace remained on the outside. Gentiles had little or no interest in the case. It was, as it appeared to the minds of men, purely a Jewish matter. Besides, Gentiles were not too numerous in the city of Jerusalem. The Roman attention was purely perfunctory as peace was maintained in this their vassal state. A few guards stood by in their cold display of duty. The followers of Jesus had been scattered. There He was, the One who had been in all eternity surrounded by the heavenly hosts, now a solitary figure standing in the weird surroundings of a criminal court. There was none to counsel; none to pity. Again, the Son of God is all alone that we might never be lonely.

Pilate put his questions in a rather erratic manner. "Art thou a king, then?" he stiffly demanded. It was here, out of the dullness of the environs, that Jesus gave us a rich, sparkling gem of glorious elucidation. "To THIS end was I born and for THIS cause came I into the world."[6] This shows something of the pointedness and positiveness of His purpose. No cup, no crown; no cross, no cure. Thus, Jesus was denounced, denied and delivered. But the enmity of the hearts of men found its most sordid display when they desired a malefactor in preference to the Master. Jesus bestowed the riches of heaven; Barabbas stole the riches of earth. Such is the deception of the human heart; such is the blindness of the depraved soul.

4Jno. 18: 39   5Acts 4: 28   6Jno. 18: 37

The Maljustice Recorded

Pilate's own confession thrice-repeated that he found no fault in Jesus should have dictated acquittal. Yet, Pilate took Jesus and scourged Him. Of what the scourging consisted and for what purpose it was imposed we are not told. Was it to intimidate Jesus? Was it to impress the angry mobs who were registering their demands? Was it to display an indication of austerity with which Rome was holding sway? This done, Pilate took a basin of water and washed his hands of the matter.[7] That in no wise disposed of the case at hand, nor did it display fairness for the One who stood at the bar of justice. Roman jurisprudence suffered irreparably that day. As for the judge, he washed his hands with a washing that only deepened the stain.

Pilate, in this act which was more dramatic than commendable, was guilty on at least five counts. (a) He bowed to popular opinion. He followed the crowd in attitude and action. He was a man, at least in this instance, of indecision. This is ill-becoming to any one when solemn decisions must be made. And what decision is more solemn than the one which comes to all, namely, "What will ye do with Jesus?" Figuratively speaking, the hand-washing episode is being emulated by the majority of earth's pilgrims down the stream of time. (b) He rested on personal pride. He felt capable of handling the matter. His mind became fixed. He must retain his position and prestige among the people whatever the cost. After all, what followers did Jesus have? A small company of despised, unlettered people, and even they had now forsaken Him or were about to do so. (c) He acted against his better judgment. He knew Christ was right both as to His manner of life and His message of love. He found no fault *in* Him and saw nothing but graciousness *about* Him. In this regard, the world at large is in perfect agreement with Pilate. Yet, against their better judgment, knowing no other name under heaven whereby they must be saved, they reject Him. (d) Pilate refused the advice of his best friend. His wife was constrained to send up to him in the

---

[7]Matt. 27: 24

midst of the weird proceedings a message, stating, "Have nothing to do with that just man: for I have suffered many things this day in a dream because of him."[8] Yet, he acquiesced to the desire of the multitudes. The best friend any man may have in this cold, cruel world of spiritual darkness and impending doom is the one who urges the right reaction toward the Saviour of men. (e) He hid behind pretense. He pretended to be wise; he pretended to be right; he pretended to be conscientious. He simply took a basin and washed his hands.

Even though Pilate's verdict was made concerning Jesus, his uncertainty and uncomfortableness are further exhibited. He returned to the Prisoner at the bar, rebuked Him and tried to force Him to speak. He revealed that, by virtue of his position, he had the power to either crucify Him or to release him. With the cool, quiet and undisturbed poise which had so perplexed Pilate throughout the trial, Jesus replied that even a Roman judge had no power of himself. He made it clear, however, that the judge was guilty, but not so much as those who had delivered Him to the judgment hall.[9] The maljustice of human jurisprudence recorded that day has never had its equal.

The Multitudes Demanding

Pilate did not send his sergeant-at-arms or the clerk of his court to report to the waiting, restless multitudes. Tension was running high. The stage was set for a revolt and it was his bounden duty to preserve the peace in the name of Rome. He would make the approach himself. He would report to them in person. He would bring Jesus before them. It was at once evident that the prolonged impatience of the milling throng could not be subdued in a moment. When silence was sufficiently established, the judge explained why he was bringing Jesus before them— "that ye may know that I find no fault in him."[10] Then Jesus appeared. Scarcely had the chief priests and the officers laid their eyes upon Him until a concerted cry arose, "Crucify him! Crucify him!"[11]

[8]Matt. 27: 19 [9]Jno. 19: 11 [10]Jno. 19: 4 [11]Jno. 19: 6

The strategy of the Jewish leaders called for the utmost
pressure to be brought to bear in order to gain their end.
"We have a law, and by our law he ought to die,"[12] they
shouted into the ears of a vacillating legalist. But should
the Jewish law supersede the Roman or even influence the
decisions of its judges? When is an occupational army
ordered about by the conquered state? Yet this was a
moment when but one custom prevailed. It was the custom
of the people to have a prisoner released at the passover.
Nor was there any question as to the prisoner who was
not to be released. They had stated their demand in a
riotous manner. Pilate sought the second time to free the
Lord Jesus, but the motley crowd cried out again, "Thou
art not Caesar's friend; whosoever maketh himself a king
speaketh against Caesar!"[13]

Pilate's position, popularity and prestige were being
threatened. He knew that Iron Caesar would give audience
to such a charge if ever it reached his ears. His decision
herewith was at once influenced. He delivered Jesus into
their hands and sat down in the judgment seat, a place
called Gabbatha. The multitude had prevailed. Jesus had
been buffetted, bound and brought. Now they could do
with Him what they would, and their plans were clearly
revealed. The *Via Dolorosa* was lengthening—Gethsemane
—Gabbatha—Golgotha.

The Mockery Displayed

The soldiers plaited a crown of thorns and placed it on
the head of Jesus. They took a purple robe and draped
it about His blessed body. This was His preparation for
presentation from Roman power to Jewish persecution. It
was sheer mockery. Then, as though this were not sufficiently humiliating, they saluted Him as the King of the
Jews, smiting Him at the same time with their hands. True
respect does not salute with the lips and smite with the
hands. This was but the prelude to pathetic indignities
which were heaped upon Him.

---

[12]Jno. 19: 7   [13]Jno. 19: 12

One can well understand that worship with the Jews lacked utterly the basic qualities of reverence and purity of heart. They were approaching the celebration of the passover, yet their hearts were filled with murder and their hands were being stained with blood. When Pilate said, "Behold your King!"[14] they reiterated their harsh demand, "Crucify him; we have no king but Caesar."[15] It is frequently stated today that this company of Jews spoke for themselves and did not express the mind of the Jewish nation. However, divine Authority says, "He came to his own and his own received him not."[16] This is one reason why the Jewish converts on the Day of Pentecost had to repent.[17] They had to change their minds about the King who was to reign over them.

"Behold the Man!" Behold the Man in His silence when wrongly accused. When He was reviled, He reviled not again. Ninety-nine people out of a hundred will retaliate when wrongly criticized or accused, but the Saviour did not. Behold the Man, Who, when He suffered, did not threaten. Can the reader imagine himself being the innocent recipient of treacherous blows without counter-attacking? Indeed, we will strike back against a preponderant force. The Lord Jesus had power to strike dead His assailants, but He preferred to speak forgiveness rather than to exercise force. Behold the Man! He is the only One upon Whom we may fix our eyes with never a disappointment.

---

[14]Jno. 19: 14   [15]Jno. 19: 15   [16]Jno. 1: 11   [17]Acts 2: 38

The Place of Penalty

"He was numbered with the transgressors"
—Isa. 53:12.

THE STRATEGY OF SATAN, amid the uproar outside the Roman court, was designed to draw Christ into the category of criminals. It would be relatively simple then for demonaical emissaries to proceed with their evil desires. "We have a law," they cried concertedly, "and by our law he ought to die!"[1]

These words struck with heavy impact upon the listening ear of the compassionate Christ and fell with even greater force upon His innocent and loving heart. It was clear that He was unwanted. The world to which He had descended with His announcement of peace and love, the world of men whom He had come to redeem, had found a law whereby He was to be violently impugned and mercilessly killed. It was the heart of depravity speaking both in word and action. The world did not want His message nor His salvation, and by vigorous manifestation proved that it did not desire Him personally. "Away with him!" they vociferously insisted.

The Pasch was coming, the notable day of Jewish celebration, the Feast of Unleavened Bread. Devout pilgrims from many nations would be entering Jerusalem in great numbers. Preparations must be completed for the Feast. As in a rush against time, Jesus was hurried to the Sanhedrin where the stoic Caiaphas put to Him the most solemn oath of the Mosaic code—the oath of testimony. He, the very embodiment of truth, is required of erring man to be accurate in His assertions. Feverishly they sought false witnesses, and, with not a little difficulty, produced two

---

[1]Jno. 19: 7

51

who feebly stated without convincing force, "This fellow said, 'I am able to destroy the temple of God, and to build it in three days.' "[2]

Alert Caiaphas, in a quick move to compensate for weakness of testimony and lack of evidence, demanded in a straightforward manner, "I adjure thee by the living God, that thou tell us whether thou be the Christ the Son of God."[3]

When Jesus calmly answered the high priest, "Thou hast said," He was neither rude nor evasive. It was a common idiom, meaning, in the parlance of the time, "I would not presume to contradict you." But the thing which riled the Jewish leader so noticeably was Jesus' comment about His ascension in power and His coming again in great glory. He began to rend his clothing—a gesture of uncontrolled irritation—and stated that there was no need for further witnesses. The fact is, none was available. Then turning to the scribes and the elders there assembled, he asked, "What think ye?"[4]

These intolerant religious bigots required no time to formulate their opinion. They were of one mind — one heart. "He is guilty of death," they coldly responded.

Being a vassal state under the jurisdiction of Rome, the Jews were restricted in their legal prerogatives. They could go no further. Their procedure thus far was of the order and character of a magistrate's court, but they had a formal demand, at least, to lay before the Roman procurator. They marked the Man of Galilee for death and delivered Him to the Roman tribunal for a verification of their own verdict and for the official invocation of penalty.

Penalty Pre-supposes Guilt

Here, as was so clearly evident in all their treatment of the Son of God, is an unsurpassed paradox. The Guiltless who came expressly for the purpose of justifying the guilty

[2]Matt. 26: 61   [3]Matt. 26: 63   [4]Matt. 26: 66

was pronounced guilty by those who posed as innocent. Human depravity prompts spurious moves and provokes nonsensical reactions.

THE OFFENSE MUST HAVE BEEN OCCASIONED. How could the Maker of immutable, divine laws be a violator? He wrote the moral law with His finger upon the tables of stone; He wrote the physical laws in the very fibre of our being; He wrote the law of His love in the very flesh of our hearts; He wrote the laws of human relationship in His eternal Word upon which all legitimate tenets of civil jurisprudence are founded. Is the Author of proper behaviour the chief offender? Also, how could a vicious criminal become a victorious Saviour? He came not to destroy but to save. He came not to condemn but to justify. He came not to violate but to fulfil. No, He was not an offender. "He had done no violence, neither was any deceit in his mouth."[5]

THE SUSPECTED CULPRIT MUST HAVE BEEN APPREHENDED. Jesus was the object of an intensive search. All schemes to apprehend Him had been frustrated heretofore because His hour had not come. Now it was different. He had drunk the cup; He had submitted Himself to the will of the Father to become the Lamb slain. But He was not a culprit. Heavily armed with swords and staves, the insurgent forces, led by Judas the betrayer, poured into the Garden of Gethsemane. There, they laid their hands upon Him. It seems so unthinkable that He who was meek and lowly of heart should be met and hounded by those so lewd and heartless.

While Jesus was humbly submissive, He was not helplessly defenceless. "Thinkest thou that I cannot now pray to my Father," He calmly inquired, "and He shall presently give me twelve legions of angels?"[6] But that the Scriptures might be fulfilled, He offered no resistance.

Almost every question which Jesus asked either went unanswered or was incorrectly attempted. "Are ye come

[5]Isa. 53: 9   [6]Mt. 26: 53

out as against a thief with swords and staves to take me?"
He queried. There was no answer. They had a law, and
He must die. So Jesus was numbered with the transgressors. He must pay the penalty, the maximum of which was
death by crucifixion. It could not be more. In this case,
it could not be less. The Scriptures must be fulfilled.

THE FACT OF GUILT MUST HAVE BEEN ESTABLISHED. To
look for imperfections in the only impeccable One this
earth ever knew would be infinitely more futile than the
proverbial task of looking for a needle in a haystack. A
needle *could* be in the hay, but no wrong inhered in the
Christ of God. But there stood Jesus before Pilate. On
the docket was the legal transcript of the Jewish trial. With
underscored emphasis, the summation stood out with bold
prominence: "We have found this man deserving of death."

With what information may be extant, together with
not a few products of their active imaginations, men have
exhausted their eloquence and literary genius to prove that
the eminent Caiaphas was scrupulously fair in the trial
of Jesus before the august body known as the Sanhedrin.
Perhaps he presided as satisfactorily as was possible. We
can almost hear him saying solemnly to his colleagues, the
judges who were squatted on the floor of that ancient,
dimly-lighted hall, "We are grappling with an unprecedented case. We must face it squarely. You have heard
the testimony. It now becomes your serious and solemn
obligation to ponder the facts in the case and to return
your honest verdict." But deliberation was unnecessary.
They called for the question in a rumbling, restless demand.
When it was put, the immediate and unanimous decision
was given. He was guilty! Should He die? The "yeas"
at once concluded the trial.

But the case was not settled. The Jewish court could
not consign Jesus to the Cross. He must go before Pilate.
Nor could Pilate accept the decision of the Sanhedrin and
acquiesce to its demand without first reviewing the evidence and formulating his own verdict. He sought to estab-

lish the fact of guilt, but failed. "I find no fault in Him," was Pilate's honest confession. But Jesus was numbered with the transgressors.

Penalty Presumes Justice

Whatever processes were employed by the Sanhedrin, whether fair or unfair, eventuated in a demand rather than a decision. It was incumbent upon Roman officialdom to hear testimony, to grant the defendant an opportunity to be heard, to examine the facts, and to render an impartial verdict which was impossible of appeal.

JUSTICE INVOLVES THE FINDINGS OF THE COURT. He Who one day will sit on the Great White Throne to find men guilty of eternal death stands now before the Roman throne of justice to hear the demand for His own execution. Whatever may be said about the thoroughness of the Jewish court, none but the careless could offer such a commendation of the Roman. In the former, it was trial by jury; in the latter, examination by judge alone. Nor does a judge usually find himself in such a precarious position. He was dealing not with one man but with many. The writhing, restless, demanding mob without constituted the threat of a serious uprising—even an alarming revolution, to say nothing of the unfavourable reaction Caesar would have to a report from the high priests if their wish were not granted.

Pilate employed intrigue, chicanery, even irony. "How can a procurator try a King?" he asked lightly, rather sparring with the determined Jewish leaders. But there was an evident uneasiness about his demeanor. As he repeatedly turned to Jesus, his questions were weak, his investigation incomplete and his attitude unbecoming. He found no fault in Jesus, yet he turned Him over to the people for crucifixion.

JUSTICE INVOLVES FIRMNESS OF THE COURT. Pilate was a veteran soldier and valiant. He was the victim of circumstances in this case. He had drawn the unfortunate assignment of maintaining law and order in a Jewish state, now Roman controlled. But there were the musty scrolls which prescribed the legal policies in the iron-clad rule of the Caesars. They could have been consulted. He might have said with unchallenged austerity, "The court finds you guilty according to the Civil Rights Act, Volume III, Article 5. In view of your premeditated and persistent violation, resulting in such serious disturbance of the peace, the court finds no alternative but to bind you over to those whom you have so grievously offended, that, according to their law, you might be duly punished for your crime." But there was no positive firmness. Nor was it necessary to remove a dusty scroll from the shelves. There was nothing inscribed therein to condemn Jesus. Pilate was bewildered —perplexed. He was more cautious about the insistence of the people than he was concerned about the interests of the prisoner. With all the indisputable power of a great conquering nation behind him, he, nevertheless, failed to speak as one who had authority.

JUSTICE INVOLVES FINALITY IN THE DECISIQN OF THE COURT. "I have power to crucify thee, and have power to release thee,"[7] Pilate informed Jesus as he returned to the judgment hall. His very attitude and intonation of voice betrayed his nervous uncertainty in the case. Yet, as the official representative of Rome, he did possess such power. He meant, as he urged upon Jesus the necessity of committing Himself, that his verdict would be final. And it was. This is the unassailable prerogative of a high court. But the decision in this instance was not fair. A true bill was not handed down. The basic facts were not produced, the testimony was perjured and justice violated. Jesus was numbered among the transgressors.

Penalty Provides Satisfaction

What did Jesus owe to the State? What did He owe to man? In what sense could He ever be in any one's debt?

---

[7]Jno. 19: 10

He is ever and always the Giver. But once again we find ourselves involved in the mysteries of our Lord's divine undertaking. He was judged in our stead. This whole matter had to do with guilt. It was our guilt. He stood in our place. In the usual prosecution of criminals, three ends must be satisfied.

THE LAW MUST BE FULFILLED. Where there is no law, or where the law is not enforced, there is anarchy in varying degrees. Each will do what is right in his own eyes. "We have a law, and by our law he ought to die," the chief priests contended! Shall we question their veracity, insofar as their having such a law is concerned! For any one to subjugate Jehovah-God by claiming to be His equal, or for any one to attempt to supplant the tenets of Judaism was considered a crime of the first order. The penalty was death. Jesus did claim to be equal with God, as indeed He was. He came also to be the end of the law for righteousness unto them that believe. He was the beginning of a new creation. He was the Substance of the shadows so characteristic of the old regime now made vague and nebulous by hoary time and the decadence of the people. But, since the veil is not taken away in the reading of the law of Moses, the Jews failed to recognize and receive their Messiah. He was rejected, condemned and numbered with the trasgressors in what they believed to be the fulfiillment of their law.

THE LAND MUST BE PROTECTED. How unfounded was Israel's fear. Well might we protect our flowers from the sunshine and our gardens from the refreshing rain. A just and devout man by the name of Simeon was waiting for the consolation of Israel and the Holy Spirit was upon him, giving to him certain clear revelations. His testimony, following the birth and circumcision of Jesus, was both sweet and simple: "Mine eyes have seen thy salvation which thou hast prepared before the face of all people; a light to lighten the Gentiles, and the glory of thy people

Israel."[8]   To kill the goose that lays the golden eggs does
not produce more eggs.   To cut off the hand that proffers
the rich blessings, does not result in more rich blessings.
Yet, the reasonings of their corrupt minds counted the rid-
dance of Jesus a protection of their land, when to them He
had brought unprecedented blessing.

THE EVIL MUST BE CURTAILED.   This is why the law
exists.   This is why it acts.   This is why culprits are sought
and seized.   Neither men nor women would find it safe
to walk the streets, much less to rest with safety in their
homes if this were not so.   But does it not stir the emotions
of dedicated hearts to think of the Lord Jesus as being
placed in such a class?   When the chief priests insisted that
He ought to die, they were saying, in substance, "We must
put an end to this evil."   Did they not like His Sermon on
the Mount?   In what sense was it destructive of peace and
unity?   Were they opposed to the blind receiving sight, the
lame empowered, the deaf having their ears unstopped?
Not exactly.   But they were fearful of the future of Judaism
if the magnetic appeal of Jesus continued to grow, causing
men in varying occupations to leave all to follow Him.
The Christian movement filled them with evil forebodings.
It must be stopped.   They must destroy the eminent Leader.
Jesus was numbered with the transgressors.

The suggestions of our subject are many.   Penalty provokes derision and presages disreputation.   It dishonours,
stigmatizes and disqualifies the convicted insofar as society
in general is concerned.   Penalty must be incurred and
invoked before it can be executed.   In the case of the Lord
Jesus, it was not personally incurred nor properly invoked,
yet it was fully executed in all the horrors and tortures of
a thousand deaths.   He was not a transgressor although He
was numbered with them.   He was the Just dying for the
unjust.[9]

8Luke 2: 30-32   91 Pet. 3: 18

The Place of Preference

"Yet it pleased the Lord to bruise him"—
Isa., 53:10.

W E NOW APPROACH the place of pleasure
—the place of God's pleasure. At first, this seems utterly
impossible, unthinkable, incredible—preposterous! Every
apparent detail would indicate the very opposite. Is there
not every sign of the displeasure of His wrath—the thunder
above, the quaking earth beneath, the darkness, the flashing
lightning? Then, too, is God like men to delight in the
suffering of another? Some of the hair-raising experiences
to which many were subjected during the days of the in-
quisitions elicited volleys of wicked glee from the depraved
onlookers. Is this our God? Was it sheer delight with Him
to view the viciousness of evil men as they meted out unspeakable treatment to His only begotten Son?

Come solemnly down highway Number 53 in the Prov-
ince of Isaiah and we will arrive at the place of pleasure.
Here, we are told, "It pleased the Lord to bruise him." I
know you do not understand it. I hope you do not understand it. I do not understand it, but my soul is subdued and
my heart veritably melts as the fact looms on the horizon of
divine revelation. We cannot be mistaken. The truth
silhouettes itself against the black background of that awful
sight. Surely the text demands both careful and prayerful
attention. Verse 9 tells us that His deeds and His words
were beyond reproach. This verse should be read with the
10th: "Because He had done no violence, neither was any
deceit in His mouth, yet it pleased the Lord to bruise Him."

Does this word *please* denote a state of ecstasy at the
sorrowful expense of another? Hardly. What then does it
mean? Perhaps an illustration will furnish us with a hint.
The moderator or chairman of a meeting asks, in parlia-
mentary parlance, "What is the pleasure of the assembly?"

Two or more matters are before them. It is incumbent upon the people to choose. Their choice indicates their preference. So it is here. All known facts establish this case: Either the Son must die or sin will reign. When we read, "It pleased the Lord to bruise him," we find that God preferred to see His Son die rather than to see sin prevail. One begins to sense something of God's holiness when one sees the unspeakable aversion and hatred with which God regards sin.

But what was the bruising? The answer necessitates the special guidance of the Spirit. We must stay very close to Him if we are to be directed into some of the successive stages of our Saviour's deep and unfathomable sorrows. Another term used in the context is, "smitten of God."[1]

Notice also the three occurrences of *grief*. In verse 3, He is "acquainted with grief." This is *contact*. The acquaintanceship was of an experiential character. At the grave of Lazarus, "He groaned in the spirit and was troubled."[2] He knew something of grief. In verse 4, we read, "Surely He hath borne *our* griefs." This is *concern*. It is more than that. That is, it led to more than that. It moved Him to do something about it, but basically it was His concern. He is concerned about our every heartache, our every problem, our every need. "Throw all your anxiety onto Him for His concern is about you."[3] In verse 10, we move from His contact with and His concern about to His *climax* in grief. "It pleased the Lord to bruise Him; He hath PUT HIM TO GRIEF." Abraham was about to put his only begotten son to death when an angel from heaven called unto him to stay his hand.[4] Here, at the Cross, no angel speaks. Heaven is not only silent, but darkened— closed! The fulness of divine wrath, the judgment which each of us deserved, was poured out on the Saviour. He suffers and dies—alone. The well must be drilled before it yields its water. The mine must be digged before it yields its nuggets. The nut must be cracked before it yields its kernel. The myrrh must be crushed before it yields its

[1]Isa. 53: 4   [2]Jno. 11: 33   [3]1Pet. 5: 7 Berkeley   [4]Gen. 22: 11

sweetness. The Son must be bruised before heaven can bestow its blessing.

The efficacy and satisfaction of Christ's work on the Cross result in several notable promises from the Father as found in our text; namely, the 10th verse of Isaiah 53. One of these we must examine. It is thus, "The pleasure of the Lord shall prosper in his hand." That is, through the nail-pierced hand of the Saviour shall proceed the unspeakable riches of God's provisions. Now do you see why it pleased the Lord God to bruise Him? To perceive His preference is to praise His matchless name. His way is the right way; His way is the best way. "Eye hath not seen, nor ear heard, neither have entered into the heart of man, the things which God hath prepared for them that love him."[5] But they are all now in the hand of the conquering Saviour for delivery to those who trust in Him. It is as though the Father said, "Son, Thou didst finish the work which I gave Thee to do. Now, I commit to Thy hand the pleasure of dispensing heaven's riches to the needy people of earth." This lends force to the words of Jesus to His discouraged people: "Fear not, little flock; for it is your Father's good pleasure to give you the kingdom."[6] What a sweeping promise! Yet, the privilege is His to grant it.

Now, we are in a position to produce some heart-stirring facts. It is the pierced hand that pours forth the blessings.

IN HIS HAND IS SALVATION. "I give unto them eternal life."[7] How multitudinous are the thoughts suggested by salvation. However vague may be one's theological conceptions, this word carries with it the thought that God has done something for us through Jesus Christ which holds out hope for all. And, of course, true hope depends upon reconciliation with God. Salvation introduces man to this vital relationship with the Almighty. It is accomplished by the Saviour becoming, through the act of faith, a vital part of us. "Christ in you the hope of glory."[8]

"Salvation is of the Lord."[9] It becomes ours by His specific gift. We do not deserve it. We cannot merit it.

[5] 1 Cor. 2: 9   [6] Luke 12: 32   [7] Jno. 10: 28   [8] Col. 1: 27   [9] Jonah 2: 9

Nor can we purchase it. But He wrought it, and He deserves to give it. This He dearly loves to do. He awaits willingness on the part of men to submit to His designs and prescriptions. Then, to as many as receive Him, He gives the power to become the sons of God. This *is* salvation and it prospers in His hand.

IN HIS HAND IS PRESERVATION. "In an acceptable time have I heard thee, and in a day of salvation have I helped thee; and I will preserve thee." To accept the Lord Jesus as one's personal Saviour is but the beginning of a new status. Its pursuant possibilities and accompanying privileges are innumerable. The new birth is an introduction into a new sphere. The preservation referred to above means *to guard.* David, in finding the Fountain of Life, exclaimed, literally, "I have begun to drink of that cup, Oh, give me rich draughts of it!" This was the joy of salvation welling up in his soul. Then, a sense of insecurity in himself gripped him and filled him with fear and alarm. Earnestly he prayed, "Let not the foot of pride come against me, and let not the hand of the wicked remove me."[10] This was a plea for the Lord to guard him in his new-found blessings. This is precisely what the pleasure of the Father is designed to do for those who cast themselves upon Him in humble dependence.

Preservation also means *to maintain.* This is what the Psalmist sought in his petition, "Quicken thou me in thy way."[11] He had a clear, understandable knowledge of life on a higher plane. He had also a deep desire and a definite determination to pursue such a course. Indeed, he had entered upon such an experience, but if he is to be maintained in it, assistance external to himself must be forthcoming. This is the thing he sought, and this the Lord delights to do. Moses reposed his faith in the assurance of this fact when he testified, "Thou in thy mercy hast led forth the people which Thou has redeemed; Thou hast guided them in Thy strength unto the holy habitation."[12]

[10]Psalm 36: 11   [11]Psalm 119: 37   [12]Ex. 15: 13

Preservation means further *to hedge in*. This is very disconcerting to the Tempter. In seeking the downfall of Job, Satan made little headway. Then he said unto the Lord, "Hast not Thou made an hedge about him?"[13] Yes, the power of preservation shall prosper in His hand.

IN HIS HAND IS SUSTENTATION. "But my God shall supply all your need according to his riches in glory by Christ Jesus."[14]

These words come to us through the experience of one who had proved the truth involved. Paul suffered hatred at its bitterest, rejection at its saddest, poverty at its depth, mockery at its worst, misunderstanding at its height, sorrow at its deepest, enmity at its fiercest, and death at its cruelist. If anybody should know about sustaining grace, Paul should be that one. He is a competent witness. One cannot name a need that has been overlooked in the wise and wonderful planning of the Lord. If it is a temptation, He provides a way of escape. If it is a sorrow, He offers comfort through the Spirit. If it is affliction, His grace is sufficient. If it is service, He fits and equips. If it is wisdom, He gives to all men liberally and upbraideth not. The means of sustentation shall prosper in His hand.

IN HIS HAND IS RESPIRATION. "In whose hand is the soul of every living thing, and the breath of all mankind."[15] "And the God in whose hand thy breath is, and whose are all thy ways, hast thou not glorified."[16]

We frequently use the expression, "As free as the air we breathe." True, it is free, but how few are the people who realize that even the air which we breathe was paid for at Calvary and now comes to us from the hand which was wounded? Someone may contend that the unChristian as well as the Christian partakes of the air without cost. The observation is correct. The rain falls on the unjust as well as on the just. There are many ways in which the rejectors of Christ benefit from His death at Calvary, but it nevertheless remains that we are indebted to the Lord

---

[13]Job 1: 10   [14]Phil. 4: 19   [15]Job 12: 10   [16]Dan. 5: 23

for our breath. "It is of the Lord's mercies that we are not consumed, because His compassions fail not."[17] It should be noticed in the quotation above, that the Lord observes with disappointment those who take their breath from Him but glorify Him not The privilege of respiration prospers in His hand.

IN HIS HAND IS MINISTRATION. "And he had in his right hand seven stars."[18] The seven stars are defined in a following verse as the messengers of the churches. The imagery indicates that He not only protects and sustains, but He despatches as well. He is the Captain of the Lord's hosts. He issues the orders. In the person of the Holy Spirit, He is the Lord of the Harvest. He gives the assignments. How wonderful to receive an ambassadorship from His blessed hand. It behooves each of us to be absolutely sure as to the place of the Lord's appointment. The authority of His ministration prospers in His hand.

IN HIS HAND IS GLORIFICATION. "Behold, I have graven thee upon the palms of my hands."[19] This is rich in suggestion. The wounds in His hands are the believers' passport to heaven, the assurance of entry there, and the cause of joyful praise upon arrival. Nor shall there be a departure from His glorious presence. The *graven palms* will prove both His purchase and His possession—eternally. They will elicit endlessly the hallelujahs of the saints. They will magnify rather than mar the beauty of His holiness. They will hallow His exaltation. They will perpetuate the perfection of His obedience. They will memorialize His incomparable love. They will answer fully the queried surprise of the celestial beings, "Who is this that cometh up from the wilderness, leaning upon her beloved?"[20] They will constitute the unchallenged reason for redeemed human renegades being received as heavenly residents.

> *"The hands of Christ were very frail,*
> *For they were broken by a nail;*
> *But only they reach heaven at last,*
> *Who are by those dear hands held fast."*

---

[17]Lam. 3: 22   [18]Rev. 1: 16   [19]Isa. 49: 16   [20]S. of S. 8: 5

The Place of Preciousness

"Ye know that ye were not redeemed with corruptible things, as silver and gold . . . but with the precious blood of Christ"— 1 Peter, 1: 18, 19.

SOME MATTERS DO NOT lend themselves to evaluation, and Calvary is the most defiant. For "none of the ransomed ever knew how deep were the waters crossed, nor how dark was the night our Lord passed through, ere He found the sheep that was lost." The transcendent values of the Cross are more evident to us than the knowledge of the cost. We cannot linger long in its shadow without finding it to be the place of preciousness.

The word *precious* is defined as "rare" or "scarce," but we are not thinking in such terms as rarity and scarcity. They do not fit the subject. We are interested in that which is absolutely without duplication, approximation or imitation. By this indefinite and indefinable standard we are to measure the immeasurable; for, until we can circumscribe Christ, we cannot circumvent the Cross.

Calvary is the place of preciousness because Christ is the personification of preciousness. "Unto you, therefore, which believe He is precious."[1]

Calvary has no duplication, for "Christ also hath *once* suffered for sins. . . ."[2]

Calvary has no approximation, for it is written, "Who is like unto thee, O Lord, among the gods? Who is like unto thee, glorious in holiness, fearful in praises, doing wonders."[3]

---

[1] Pet. 2: 7   [2] 1Pet. 3: 18   [3] Ex. 15: 11

Calvary is without imitation, for "there is none other name under heaven given among men whereby we must be saved."[4]

Remember, it was the Master, not the malefactors, who made Calvary meaningful and immortal.

Go to the Battlefield of Gettysburg and the guides will say, "Brave men died here for the preservation of national unity." Go to the Marne, to Chateau-Thierry or to Verdun, and they will tell you, "Valiant men laid down their lives here to make the world safe for democracy." Go to Northern Africa, Western Europe, the islands of the Pacific, and you will be informed that gallant men paid the supreme sacrifice to insure lasting peace.

Now, go to Calvary and the Holy Spirit will reveal that the Lord of Glory laid down His life that the rebel sons of Adam's race might have life eternal. This makes Calvary precious, for it is a precious place indeed when we know that life itself, and that for eternity, issues therefrom.

There are certain substantiating facts which magnify the preciousness of Calvary. For instance, as sparkling jewels against the black background of man's sinful record, there shine forth three transcendent truths, namely, His love, His blood, His grace. The depth of His love moved Him to shed his blood and the efficacy of His blood provided the riches of His grace. Behind the blood, the love, and through the blood, the grace. What did it cost? We cannot know. Christ was God's kohinoor diamond, heaven's most precious gem, and the Cross was the spectrum which diffused the radiant glory of His love and the luminous energy of His grace.

The stated reason why the Saviour was the Good Shepherd is that He laid down His life for the sheep. Can we count the cost of this? It was a voluntary act; it was a vital operation. "Without the shedding of blood is no remission."[5] But the rigours of the Cross cannot be defined. There is no profitable point in speculating about His suf-

---

[4]Acts 4: 12   [5]Heb. 9: 22

ferings. The dramatic, too, is decidedly irrelevant in the portrayal of this solemn and significant event.

The Place Where His Precious Love Was Proved

THE EXTENT OF HIS LOVE. If we have the right perspective, we must agree that He went to the Cross to provide, not to prove. But the fact that He went nevertheless produced many proofs. Not the least of these was the assurance of His love. "Greater love hath no man than this, that a man lay down his life for his friends."[6] When Jesus wept at the grave of Lazarus, the mourning Jews exclaimed, "Behold how he loved him!"[7] At the Cross, rejoicing hearts cry, "Behold, how He loved *all!*"

True love suffers long and is kind. It does not waver because of weariness. It does not forget its task because the going is difficult. It does not fear the consequences when duty calls. It leaps to the opportunity of serving, and welcomes the privilege of suffering, if need be, that beneficial ends for others may be attained. It does not delay because of the darkness and wish for the light. Nor does it wait for the tidal-wave to subside before plunging into the engulfing waters. It surmounts the hindering barriers with no thought of self-sacrifice, and faces death with a daring dauntlessness. This is the portrait of true love, and no love was truer than our Lord's. Man's love is relative; Christ's love is absolute.

THE FULNESS OF HIS LOVE. The corona of the *aurora borealis* in the realm of heavenly revelation centred in the truth of John 3:16, "For God so loved the world, that he gave his only begotten Son, that whosoever believeth in Him should not perish, but have everlasting life." On the one side was an eternal God with His great love. On the other, a lost humanity with its inevitable doom, and a gaping chasm between. The hand of mercy which is not shortened that it cannot save,[8] extended a love from God's heart to the helpless souls on the other side, and the gap was bridged. Here Calvary stands in the plan of the ages.

---

[6]Jno. 14: 15   [7]Jno. 11: 36   [8]Isa. 59: 1

The Cross is the passage-way from death to life; and when faith takes the hand of the Saviour, He leads unerringly to a refuge where death hath no more dominion.

In all our lingering at Calvary, perhaps we are at no time more helpless than when we attempt to survey the fulness of the Saviour's love. Calvary must speak for itself. Nor is it a mute testimony. It is vibrant and vital in its expression. It speaks volumes. In the twinkling of an eye faith sees that it is love divine, all love excelling. This puts us in the sphere of infinity, and eternity itself will be too brief to reveal fully the exhaustless expanses of His wonderful affection. It envelops men of all ages from Adam on down through the great human race, and still leaves ample room for the limitless "whosoever" invitation to all the tribes and nations until the day dawn and the shadows flee away. The Cross becomes the artesian well of the heart of God, and from it gushes the fulness of His unchanging love.

The Place Where His Precious Blood Was Poured

THE DECLARATION OF HIS SHED BLOOD. "This cup is the new covenant in my blood, which is SHED for you."[9] It is hardly accurate to say, as is frequently heard, that Jesus spilled His blood on the Cross. That does not give the sense. It was *shed* or *poured*, and herein is a matter of great magnitude. The blood of the ancient sacrifices, as prescribed by the Lord through Moses, was poured beside the bottom of the altar.[10] The anointing oil was poured so profusely that it ran down over Aaron's beard and onto his garments.[11] Such other things are poured as wrath, indignation, fury and blessings. The same word is used for the descent of the Holy Spirit in His present administration. The Lord declared that His blood would be shed—that there was to be a complete outpouring of His life for the world. This was proved at Calvary.

THE DEMAND FOR HIS SHED BLOOD. "Without shedding of blood is NO remission."[12] The demand could be satis-

[9]Lu. 22: 20 [10]Ex. 29: 12 [11]Psalm 133: 2 [12]Heb. 9: 22

fied only by a complete yielding of the life of Jesus. He must die as the Just One if the unjust ones were to be justified. He did not merely swoon. He died; He gave up the ghost. His life was laid down. Anything short of this would have failed to satisfy the claims. Either He must die, or we must die. As our Substitute, He died. He shed His blood; He poured it forth. Since the life is in the blood,[13] the shedding of His blood was the pouring forth of His life. This is why His blood is called precious. This is why we sing, "What can wash away my sin? Nothing but the blood of Jesus."

The Place Where His Precious Grace Was Provided

When the music of God's grace has impressed its harmony on a human heart, heavenly anthems become vibrant in the soul. Nor can the temple of man retain its strains. It creeps through the crevices of his every expression. Perhaps no life apart from that of our Lord Jesus has given truer tones than the Apostle Paul's, the lovely echoes of which have been dominant on the ether waves of time down through all these centuries. Yet, every one who has tasted of His grace should have a joyfulness within, and there is no better way to get started in the right key than to linger at Calvary.

GRACE IS SUBLIME. When they smote the Saviour, they struck the Rock whence flowed the Water of Life. When they tacked His hands to the Cross, they tapped heaven's resources. When they pierced His side, they penetrated the power of God. Grace looms transcendently glorious above all the forces known to man. Indeed, one stands in helpless awe before its indefineably momentous scope. It is fathomless in fact and limitless in force. It is sweetly freighted with the fragrance of heaven and filled with the fulness of omnipotence. Behind the now impenetrable mists of futurity there awaits a glorious revelation of the exceeding greatness of His grace.[14] However, it is marvelous in its present manifestations and miraculous in its manifold

---

[13]Lev. 17: 14 [14]Eph. 2: 7

operations.[15]   Its freeness to undeserving sinners melts
hearts into deep contrition and lifts the lost into the realm
of incomparable blessing.

HIS GRACE IS SUFFICIENT. "My grace is sufficient for
thee."[16] How disconsolate and forlorn is the sinner! What
misery, confusion and horror are—bound in the prison
walls of sin to grope about in his dungeon of darkness. And
that is precisely where we all would be had there been no
Calvary. Jesus said, "If the light that is in thee be darkness, how great is that darkness."[17] Yet, the depravity of
man prefers darkness to light.

Not only was the region of Zebulun and Naphthali
flooded with the "Sun of Glory," but every believer has had
a *golden daybreak*. Through the mercy of God, the Day-
spring has visited us with deliverance from darkness and
an introduction into the kingdom of His dear Son. This is
the message of Calvary to the trusting heart. The grace
here made possible is transforming in its truth and satisfying in its wonderful sufficiency. As light suits the eye and
as truth fits the conscience, so grace meets the need of the
soul of man. Its rays of light are lovelier than the fairest
sunset, while its music is a doxology with an ever-increasing
crescendo. Grace is matchless in its appeal.

HIS GRACE IS SUPERABUNDANT. "But where sin abound-
ed, grace did much more abound."[18] Though Israel was
sailing the sea of forgetfulness and disobedience, Jehovah
stood entreatingly on the shore of faithfulness and love. His
voice swept over the waves of unbelief and His hand was
stretched out invitingly.[19] In the prophecy of Hosea alone
He calls endearingly for the return of His people no less
than a score of times, most of which invitations were grievously unheeded. Echoing through the centuries, and
sweetly resounding in this day of grace, is the same loving
voice. Jesus is tenderly calling today. He bids men to
come to His bountiful storehouse and buy without money
and without price.

---

[15]1 Pet. 4: 10   [16]2 Cor. 12: 9   [17]Mk. 6: 23   [18]Rom. 5: 20   [19]Prov. 1: 24

When we get to our wit's end—and it does not take us long to arrive there—we may fix our eyes upon God. He will never suffer the righteous to be moved. He knows our need before we ask, and grants our request when we ask in faith believing. He will never under any circumstances leave us in the lurch. He promises His presence, provides His power and protects His people. We may cast our every weight upon Him, for He that delivered, does deliver and we may trust Him yet to deliver. The sun stood still, the axe did swim—*this* God is our God!

Calvary is the place of preciousness because it became the outlet, through Christ's sufferings, for the divine supplies which are so sorely needed by bankrupt humanity. Nor was there any other way to furnish this realm with these vital necessities.

The Place of Provision

"What are these wounds in thine hands?"—
Zech. 13:6.

THERE ARE TWO LINES of Biblical prediction concerning the Lord Jesus Christ which stand out on the Sacred Page with about equal prominence. One relates to His sufferings; the other to His glory. The meditations of this volume have to do almost exclusively with His sufferings. However, the text at hand leads both lines of truth into one focus. The King in all His beauty will come with wounds in His hands. "Behold he cometh with clouds; and every eye shall see him, and they also which pierced him; and all kindreds of the earth shall wail because of him."[1]

The Holy Spirit employs the interrogation unerringly throughout the Scriptures. The question before us registers at once; but that we may have it more firmly fixed in our minds, we shall ponder each word briefly. *First*, there is apparent surprise—"What!" *Second*, there is continuing manifestation—"are." *Third*, there is proof of purposed infliction as suggested by the demonstrative—"these." *Fourth*, there is perpetual evidence that the One Who comes in His glory is the same One Who died on the Cross—"wounds." *Fifth*, there is the personal possession of these eternal evidences—"thine." *Sixth*, the parts of His blessed body which were pierced—"hands." Some have gone to no little effort in an attempt to prove that the Saviour's hands only were nailed to the Tree, and this in spite of our Lord's own words to His disciples in one of His post-resurrection appearances, "Behold my hands AND MY FEET."[2] Per-

---

[1]Rev. 1: 7 [2]Luke 24: 39

73

haps reference elsewhere is made to His hands only because they were prominently stretched forth in invitation.

But it is the matter of wounds which stands out in our present consideration. The question concerns His wounds. And let us bear in mind that they were not scars! They were wounds. The writer has carried with him the evidence of an accident which transpired in childhood while playing with a sharp knife. Then it was a wound; now it is a scar. Not so with the Lamb of God Who was slain by wicked hands. They are still wounds. There is something fresh about them, something availing. Let us look at the word acrostically:

> **W** illingness.
> **O** mnipotence.
> **U** nderstanding.
> **N** ecessity.
> **D** eliverance.
> **S** atisfaction.

The first three thoughts suggested by the acrostic pertain primarily to the Saviour; the second three to mankind, yet all concern Him. His offering for sin was a voluntary one. He submitted to it willingly. It called for supernatural power to deal with such a treacherous enemy as Satan, but He had power to lay down His life and power to take it again. This is omnipotence. And what shall we say of His understanding? He knew all the considerations involved in the rescue of sinners. Had there been a better way, He would have found it. Our great necessity for a salvation which would lift us out of hopeless despair brought Him from the Throne above. He was the one and only Deliverer who could assure victory over sin and the grave. He was the only One who could satisfy all the rigorous requirements of the law and inexorable justice of an Holy God.

But what are these wounds in His hands? David, by inspiration, saw a cup in His hand.[3] It was the cup which

---

[3] Psalm 75: 8

Jesus took when His soul was exceeding sorrowful unto death. John the Baptist, by inspiration, saw a fan in His hand.[4] He envisioned the Lord purging His floor, separating the chaff from the wheat. Isaiah, by inspiration, saw a welcome in His hand.[5] These were days of rebellion and apostasy, but, behind the dim unknown, God was faithfully standing in the shadow, keeping watch above His own. His hands of love were ever outstretched to a disobedient people. But what are these wounds in His hands?

In His hands a sceptre was placed.[6] It is a sceptre of righteousness. Into His hand all government shall be given.[7] Into His hand all judgment is committed.[8] In his hand all power both in heaven and earth is vested.[9] But what are these wounds in His hands?

THE SYMBOL OF SALVATION. The Lord Jesus had glory with the Father before the world was. He made the mountains, designed the deeps, shaped the shrubs, outlined the oceans—in wisdom He made them all.[10] How could He turn from the glorious to the inglorious? How could He meet and mingle with the creatures He had created? How could He climb mountains He had made? Or plant His feet on fields that fell from His fingers? That is, how could the exalted One become so humbled? Condescension with Christ was glorious when He was doing His Father's will, and this He came to do. He came to seek and to save that which is lost. This was the transcendent purpose in His condescending presence among men.

The wounds in His hands give the believer standing before God. When the adversary accuses the brethren night and day before the Throne, the wounds of the Advocate symbolize the efficacy of His work on Calvary. They are there, and the Devil knows why they are there; he knows when they were put there. They made possible our salvation.

THE PROOF OF SUBSTITUTION. "He was wounded for *our* transgressions, He was bruised for *our* iniquities; the

4Matt. 3: 12   5Isa. 64: 2   6Heb. 1: 8   7Isa. 9: 6   8Acts 10: 42
9Matt. 28: 18   10Psalm 104: 24

chastisement of our peace was upon Him."[11]   He had done
no violence; there was no deceit in His mouth. The Roman
judge could find no fault in Him. Nor is this to be wondered at when God, on the mount of transfiguration, had
thoroughly inspected His Lamb before He went to the
slaughter. It is concluded, therefore, that He suffered not
for Himself but for others.

In the realm of ungodliness is a trio of death-dealing
monsters, namely, transgression, iniquity and sin. David
penitently confessed guilt on all three of these counts in his
immortal repentance of Psalm 51. Transgression, as the
word suggests, is a running crosswise to the Word and will
of God. Briefly, it is rebellion against God. Iniquity is an
inward perversion, and sin is missing the mark. The Lord
Jesus, in His substitutionary death was wounded for our
transgressions, was bruised for our iniquities and was
chastened for the peace-destroying sin which fills the lives
of men.

Those who recognize and receive by faith the value of
His finished work become the recipients of His accomplishments. We should rejoice with Micah, saying, "Who is a
God like unto thee, that pardoneth iniquity, and passeth by
the transgression . . . and will cast all their sins into the
depths of the sea."[12] The substitutionary work of Christ
has made it possible for the Infinite God to pardon iniquity,
pass transgression, withdraw his anger and delight in show-
ing mercy. He will hear; He will have compassion; He
will subdue iniquity; He will bury our sins. The wounds
in His hands provide the proof of this.

THE MARK OF IDENTIFICATION. "And it came to pass.
. . ." This is the introduction to the advent announcement.
With what glorious certainty the Holy Spirit proclaims the
glad tidings! With added significance, Jesus informed men
that "the Son of man IS come." He came from somewhere,
yet who but the blessed Holy Spirit can tell us whence?
Once in the ivory palaces; now, nowhere to lay His head.
Once with garments perfumed with aloes, cassia and myrrh;

---
[12]Micah 7: 18, 19 [11]Isa. 53: 5

now, with robes to become soiled by sinful hands as villains tore them from His body, parting His garments by casting lots. But, bless His name, He came!

He came to identify Himself with mankind, to make all that was theirs His that He might make all that was His theirs. He walked among men, ate and slept with them, rode their beasts of burden and sailed the seas in their ships. He healed and helped, blessed and promised. He descended to the earth as our Emmanuel and went to the Cross to become our Emancipator. The body in which He made His advent will be His eternally, and the wounds which men inflicted upon that body will be evident for ever. These wounds will always be a testimony to His identification with humanity.

THE SHELTER OF SECURITY. "Rock of ages, cleft for me, let me hide myself in Thee." Whether in these words or in others, whether uttered or unexpressed, this is the first song that faith sings when the Spirit reveals to man his great need of the Saviour. What are these wounds in His hands? They are His welcome. As the impending judgment was nearing, a voice within the ark said to Noah, "Come thou and all thy house into the ark."[13] This is precisely the message of the wounds. They invite unsheltered men to refuge where the nearer waters cannot engulf, where the blasts of bitter judgment cannot hurt or harm.

When we read about the great day of God's wrath in the which no one will be able to stand, we should be deeply grateful for the wounds in His hands. When we read about the heavens departing and the mountains and the islands being removed out of their places, we should rejoice that we are sheltered. When we read of the futile prayers of the kings of the earth, the great men, the rich and the chief captains who, seeking death and cannot find it, call for the rocks and the mountains to fall on them, we should praise God for the wounds in the Saviour's hands. One glimpse of a lost eternity with all its disillusionment and misery,

---

[13]Gen. 7: 1

and we should humble ourselves in much reverential worship with an attendant gratitude which is true and unaffected, knowing that we are sheltered in His wounds.

THE RECEIPT OF HIS PURCHASE. This sufferings were the price of our redemption; the wounds were His receipt that the price had been paid. It was a price concerning which He was thoroughly conscious, but from paying it He shrank not for a single moment. The value of your soul and mine He esteemed worth it all. He would do it again were it needful, but praise His name, it is not necessary. The great transaction was adequately met and forever settled. He sustained the serpent's sting, absorbed its venom, took the crushing force of the law, faced the condemnation of men, and died ignominiously. He trod the winepress of God's wrath, tasted of its fierceness; and, gathering up in His bosom the very paroxysms of hell, He cried out victoriously, "It is finished!" His wounds constitute the receipt for the finished transaction.

In the western part of Canada, in a small and humble dwelling, lives a woman all alone. In a conversation at her door, a missionary learned something of the circumstances which surround her life. Her husband was killed in World War I. The indemnity which she had received was used partly to provide the small home, the balance being used to procure the necessities of life. Said she, in a solemn tone, "You see, I am living on my husband's wounds."

In a very true sense, every Christian is living on the wounds of Christ. How poorly we realize this. We recall the words of Count Zinzendorf when he was requested to give the charge to a Moravian missionary who was being sent to the field. With stately mien, he walked to the platform and respectfully put two questions to the young man. "Brother John, dost thou know His wounds? Hast thou entered into the merits thereof?" That was all, but that was profound. We need to know His wounds; we need so sorely to enter into the merits thereof. He was wounded; we are welcomed. He was blasted; we are blessed. He was humiliated; we are exalted. The bride is received home without spot or blemish, while the Bridegroom carries the wounds throughout eternity.

The world has its allurements, and sin vaunts its pleasures. Multitudes have been both intrigued and entrapped thereby; but one clear view of Calvary—its cost, its love, its hope, then there can be but one heart utterance:

> *"Were the whole realm of nature mine*
> *That were a present far too small;*
> *Love so amazing, so divine*
> *Demands my soul, my life, my all."*

The Place of Prayer

"Father, forgive them; for they know not what they do"—Luke 23:34.

W E SHOULD BE GRATEFUL ALWAYS, even beyond possible expression, for the "new and living way"[1] which has been opened for us into the presence of God. And we must remember that Calvary has made possible this blessed privilege. How can we forget the incalculable price which was paid to establish the *new way* and to give virility to the erstwhile mute symbols of the ceremonial procedure? The glorious ascension of our Great High Priest into the Holy of Holies at the Father's right hand may not have been without fearful conflict. It is believed that the Prince of the power of the air, with his collaborating cohorts, ambushed our Lord's journey upwards. But our Forerunner has entered in! In doing so, He has established for His people constant access to the Throne of Grace.

The *old way* made obligatory an intricate procedure, one which became wearisome to God's ancient people in their declining spiritual state. "They walked mournfully before the Lord of hosts."[2] Perhaps we are too far removed, or too poorly instructed, to appreciate the actual involvements of ancient Jewish worship. If we could more thoroughly comprehend in detail the ancient ceremonial procedure, perhaps we would value more highly the "new and living way" which is ours under the new covenant. Christ, in His life and death, fulfilled in detail every suggestion of the Mosaic symbols. While the lightbeams of truth in the five Levitical Offerings seem to shine out di-

---

[1]Heb. 10: 20   [2]Mal. 3: 14

vergently, they finally converge at Calvary. The pictorial
emphases in these former object lessons become very real
at the Cross.

No well-informed person would picture the Brazen Altar
as a thing of beauty from the standpoint of its appearance
and operation. Nor would one concede that the Cross was
exactly aesthetic. Try to visualize the Brazen Altar as it
is being used in the ceremonial order. Witness the curling
clouds of blackened smoke rising high into the otherwise
clear atmosphere. Note the offensive odor of burning flesh
as it is being consumed by the fire. Does it commend itself
to the reader's aesthetic nature as a sightly scene upon
which to gaze with deep and evident pleasure? Hardly.
Nor is the Cross more inviting to the vision or pleasant to
the emotions. It was a ghastly thing—a hideous instrument to inflict the most excruciating suffering upon human
beings.

But we must proceed from the Brazen Altar and observe
that, between the place of sacrifice with its attendant un-
pleasantness and the Holy of Holies was the Altar of Incense. This was always pleasing to Jehovah when the
incense was proper and the fire not strange. When was the
incense proper? There were two requirements to make it
so. *First*, it must be sweet. "And Aaron shall burn thereon SWEET incense every morning."[3] *Second*, it must be
pure. "And he made the holy anointing oil, and the PURE
incense of sweet spices."[4]

When we turn to the New Testament scene, we learn
that incense is associated with prayer. Indeed, it is a
symbol of prayer. "According to the custom of the priest's
office, his lot was to burn incense when he went INTO the
temple of the Lord. And the whole multitude of the people
was praying WITHOUT at the time of incense."[5] The incense was figurative; the praying was actual. Prayer that
is proper, sweet and pure, ascends from the soul of man
to the heart of God as a sweet-smelling savour. In a very
solemn setting, we note another corroborating association

[3]Ex. 30: 7   [4]Ex. 37: 29   [5]Lu. 1: 9, 10

of incense and prayer: "And another angel came and stood
at the altar, having a golden censer; and there was given
unto him much incense, that he should offer it with the
prayers of all saints upon the golden altar which was before
the Throne. And the smoke of the incense with the prayers
of the saints ascended up before God."[6]

Of all the ignominy of that gory scene at the Place of
the Skull—the shame which our Lord so deeply despised—
we lose a tremendous blessing if we fail to recognize the
incense. Despite the curse of the crucifixion, the stamped-
ing of the bulls of Bashan, the noxiousness of their vituperation, the mockery of the thorny crown, to say nothing of
pain, the Lord Jesus Christ hallowed the spot with a prayer
of touching significance. Amid all the unsavoury aspects
of the scene, there went from His blessed lips the sweet
and pure incense of prayer, as between the Brazen Altar
and the Holy of Holies.

The Incense of Forgiveness

"Father, forgive them, for they know not what they
do."[7] In all manner of communication, Jesus spake as never
man spake, and how transcendently gracious were the
words of this intercessory prayer. With what delicate intonation His bleeding heart sent forth the articulate plea.
It involved a restored fellowship with the Father, a full forgiveness for His assailants, and a recognized ignorance on
the part of those who heaped indignities upon Him.

A RESTORED FELLOWSHIP. When did we last hear the
Master pray? Was it when the rabble crew, ruffians of the
baser sort, laid their wicked hands upon Him to bring Him
bound into the judgment hall? No. Was it when He stood
in His own humble innocence to be interrogated by Pilate
while the multitudes without were agitating wildly for His
death? No. Was it when He was mockingly presented
to the blood-thirsty throngs with a crown of thorns pressed
upon his bleeding brow and a purple robe enshrouding

6Rev. 8: 3, 4   7Lu. 23: 34

Him? No. Was it while He walked the *Via Dolorosa* bearing the heavy Cross along the winding path to the place of execution? No. Was it when He stretched forth His blessed hands to have the spikes driven with unbearable pain through the fibres of His human body? No. When, then, was it?

From the time Jesus prayed in the Garden of Gethsemane that the cup might pass from Him, until these last moments on the Cross, we do not read that He prayed. Even though the series of events developed in rapid succession, there is an eternity of significance to His lack of communion with the Father. Only after prayerful and careful pondering do we venture a suggestion. In dark Gethsemane, He had a cup in His hand. What was that cup?

Sometime prior to His appearance in Pilate's judgment hall, Jesus was "made sin for us, who knew no sin; that we might be made the righteousness of God in Him."[8] Are we able to put our finger on the time when this imputation took place? It must have been in the Garden. If in the Garden, the anteroom of Golgotha, then it must have been when He took the cup. He did not, as some would suppose, shrink from the Cross. He knew the end from the beginning. He was in the council of planning, according to Psalm 85:10. Was He not the Lamb slain from before the foundation of the world? From what, then, did He shrink? If we are justified in calling it a shrinking, then it was from contact with despicable sin—the sin of the world as it touched His holy nature.

If He was made sin, then He lost fellowship with the Father. He was not condemned, but He took the guilt of the condemned and stood in the place of the condemned. The condemned have no fellowship with God. He was not a sinner, but He was, by voluntary substitution, in the position of a sinner; and "God heareth not sinners."[9] Thus, in a manner utterly incomprehensible to us, Jesus trod the winepress all alone. Having shared the glory of the Father in eternity past, can we even begin to appreciate the inex-

[8]II Cor. 5: 21   [9]Jno. 9: 31

pressible suffocation of soul which closed in upon Him in this hour of terrible grief, being cut off from the Father. This accounts for the surging soul outburst in the ninth hour, "My God, my God, why hast thou forsaken me?"[10]

During the three hours of *eons* of indescribable suffering, the work which He so decidedly desired to finish reached its completion. The law was fulfilled; the justice of God was vindicated; the salvation for men was assured. Then, and only then, as it would seem to our finite and faulty discernment, the Father smiled again with glorious approval upon His beloved son. Sin was put away by the death of Himself. The darkness disappeared and heaven opened to His view. Fellowship was restored. Then He could pray. Then He did pray.

A FULL FORGIVENESS. Jesus asked the Father to forgive His vile persecutors. Is this not the essence of Scripture to forgive them that despitefully use you? Is this not the spirit of Calvary where divine forgiveness was made possible? How fitting was this intercession? If Christ's bitter suffering did not produce a work sufficient to cover the crimes of those so near to the Cross, it would not be sufficient for our sins. If it was sufficient for theirs, it *is* sufficient for ours. Calvary's power began at once to flow forth in Niagaras of forgiveness, and who seemed to be the least worthy but those who so violently and so flagrantly heaped unspeakable indignities on such a loving Saviour.

There is of course the further example of the believing malefactor. He was no nearer than the transgressor on the opposite cross. Nor was he more worthy, but he did acknowledge the Lord. This at once opens the floodgates of Calvary. "That if thou shalt CONFESS WITH THY MOUTH the Lord Jesus, and shalt believe in thine heart that God hath raised Him from the dead, thou shalt be saved."[11] Our part is so simple, but, if sincere, the potency of the Cross goes to work and never fails to produce a new status for the trusting soul.

[10]Matt. 27: 46   [11]Rom. 10: 9, 10

A KNOWLEDGE OF THEIR IGNORANCE. "They know not what they do," the Saviour graciously explained. Such ignorance cannot be construed as innocence. They were guilty and condemned, and, without the finished work of Christ applied, would be lost eternally. But so far as putting Christ to death was concerned, those who drove the nails in His hands and feet, and planted the cross and pierced His side, were no more guilty than any sinner of any day. Our sins as well as theirs put Him there. Of those who participated in the crucifixion of Christ, not one will have to answer at the Great White Throne for the cruel deeds of that particular day. Why? Because the dying Saviour asked the Father to forgive them for what they had done. The Apostle Paul, by divine unction, contended that, "had they known it, they would not have crucified the Lord of glory."[12] But they did crucify Him; yet He freely forgave them. Was not His prayer from the Cross, under such conditions, the richest of incense?

The Incense of Confident Submission

Do keep in mind the required characteristics of the incense which was used in the tabernacle of old. It was to be sweet and pure. Then it was acceptable to Jehovah. Are not these chief characteristics most evident in the delicate loveliness of our Saviour's praying on Calvary?

THE SWEETNESS OF HIS CONFIDENCE. "Father, into Thy hands I commend my spirit."[13] It was the confidence of a perfect fulfilment of plans. It was the confidence of the Father's fullest approval. It was the confidence of a future pleasure, "who for the joy that was set before him, endured the cross, despising the shame."[14] It was the confidence of presenting many sons in the glory. He now puts His spirit in the hands which so lately had poured out wrath upon Him.

THE PURITY OF HIS REVERENCE. It is not now, "My God! My God! why hast thou forsaken me?" No, it is

[12]1 Cor. 2: 8 [13]Lu. 23: 46 [14]Heb. 12: 2

"Father, Thou hast shown Thy blessed face. Ere My body descends to the grave, into Thy hands commend I my Spirit." And because we are sons, Paul informs us, God has sent forth the Spirit of his Son into *our* hearts, crying, "Abba, Father."[15]   What purity *we* have is resultant from the fact of Christ being in us. Whatever reverence we may evidence toward God is due to the Spirit's operation through us. With the Saviour, the purity of incense always permeated His life and ministry. He is not only the essence of purity but the substance of it.

We cannot venture far into this precious aspect of the Cross, but in the fearful struggle, it is not difficult to believe that the cohorts of Satan had barricaded the way to the Throne of God. Is this not equally true of the saints as well? We wrestle to work; we relax to worship; but the fiercest battles rage when the humble suppliant bends his knee to pray.

---

[15]Gal. 4: 6

The Place of Peace

". . . having made peace through the blood of his cross"—Col. 1:20.

P EACE IS SECOND ONLY to love in sweetness, sound and significance. But what makes it so amazingly wonderful? What gives to it such incomparable qualities? Simply this—peace is of God. "God is not the author of confusion but of peace."[1] Earth may languish in the bitterness of conflict but all heaven lies in the calmness of a settled restfulness, in the serenity of wholesome and joyful harmony. Thieves cannot break through to steal. Fiends cannot foment insurrections. Nor can foes foster strife.

What is peace, then, but the atmosphere of heaven. It is sometimes difficult to distinguish between the processes and the products in the divine economy, but peace we know to be the result of justification;[2] and justification is the result of the perfectness and the completeness of Christ's work on the cross, divinely approved, as shown by His resurrection from the grave.

Peace is said to be perfect union between two personalities. In this regard, we observe with interest the distinction between "peace with God" and the "peace of God." The former is the result of accepting; the latter is the reward of abiding. As soon as one comes to the crossroads of life and faces the greatest of all issues, that of personal salvation, and accepts Christ as the only One under heaven who can meet man's every need, at once that one is set at peace with God. The rebellion ceases, selfish designs end, and the way of the Lord becomes pleasingly acceptable. Then one is at peace with God. But those who find the way of life

[1] Cor. 14: 33   [2] Rom. 5: 1

in truth and assurance are called upon to continue in the faith, to grow in grace and to mature in spiritual matters. Through obedience and yieldedness comes the constant blessing of the peace *of* God which garrisons the hearts of saints amid the conflicts of life.

Lingering at Calvary in the shadow of the Cross furnishes us with something of the fact, the factors, and the focus of peace. We find that God is the Author of peace;[3] that its character is of absolute perfection;[4] that its design is to reconcile;[5] that its operation is to keep the hearts and minds of believers;[6] that it is a present of Christ;[7] that it is the promoter of unity;[8] that its realization is present and partial, future and full.

The Purchaser—"He"

HIS PERSONAL ATTENTION. Some matters in the divine scheme of things are allocated to the archangel, others to the ministering spirits, some to cherubim, still others to men; but there are some things which the Lord Jesus must reserve for Himself. "*I* go to prepare a place for you," He said, "*I* will receive you unto myself." No one can substitute for Him in these matters. The same was true concerning Calvary. Righteous Enoch, faithful Noah, obedient Moses, dedicated Joshua, fully-surrendered Elijah — not one could grapple with the powers of hell and endure the wrath of God to effect so great a salvation for mankind. No, Jesus alone could satisfy the exacting claims. This point was strongly emphasized by Him in His teaching: "The Son of man MUST suffer many things, and be rejected of the elders, and of the chief priests, and be killed."[9]

He, Himself, made peace through the blood of His cross. Note the PERSONALITY—"He." The spotlight of Scripture is ever focused upon Christ. His personality shines through its pages with glistening grandeur and sparkling splendour. Observe the VITALITY — "the blood." No less a price would do. He MUST lay down His

[3]Heb. 13: 20   [4]Isa. 26: 3   [5]Col. 1: 20   [6]Phil. 4: 7
[7]Jno. 14: 27   [8]Psalm 133: 1   [9]Mark 8: 31

life. The word "must" is one of the strongest in the whole
vocabulary of man. It breathes the very essence of com-
pulsion. There are certain things we do because of sheer
delight. There are other things we refrain from doing
because of utter detestation. There are some things we
MUST do whether pleasurable or distasteful. Even the Son
of God had the lash of the *must* about His blessed head.
"He must needs go through Samaria."[10] He *must* be rejected—killed. But His rejection brought our acceptance;
His death made possible our life. Witness also the INSTRU-
MENTALITY—"His cross". It was the middle cross which
broke down the "middle wall of partition".[11] It was this
instrument of death which slew the enmity of hearts. Real
peace came out of a tempest, but Jesus Himself in the midst
of the raging battle won the day and wrought the peace.

HIS PATIENT ALERTNESS. Without meter or measuring
rod, our ever-present Lord knows the fluctuations of our
emotions. He witnesses the surges of the soul. "Somebody
knows when our heart aches, and everything seems to go
wrong." It was from His own dear lips that earth's sweetest
benediction came. To weeping, wilting and wearying souls,
He graciously whispered, "Peace I leave with you. My
peace I give unto you; not as the world giveth, give I unto
you. Let not your heart be troubled, neither let it be
afraid."[12] Then and there, divine peace, supernal quietude,
became the present of Christ. Nor has it ever lessened in
its offer or value. It is not a sedative to soothe for the
moment, but a remedy to relieve for ever. It is the answer
of the Good Shepherd to the bleating, bleeding and broken
members of the flock. It is the announcement of the Saviour
to the fearful, fainting disciples of His calling. It is the
comfort of the Spirit to the sorrowing souls of the saints.

HIS POWERFUL ACCOMPLISHMENT. Just as the tempest-
tossed sailors preferred to bail out the water rather than to
believe in the wonderful Saviour, so men of all ages turn
from the Cross to their conferences for peace. The struggles
have been valiant and the intentions commendable, but the

[10]Jno. 4: 4   [11]Eph. 2: 14   [12]Jno. 14: 27

Utopian goal of millenia of hoping is today more remote than ever. Skillful diplomacy has failed; political intrigue has fallen short of the mark; and devastating weapons have produced harm but not harmony among the nations. Jesus not only promised peace; He provided it. He is the Prince of Peace.

The Provision—"Peace"

A restless, writhing, reckless humanity needed, and still needs, as nothing else, this soothing, sustaining and supernatural product of Calvary.

IT IS EXCLUSIVE IN ITS ORIGIN. Jesus made it unmistakably clear that the peace which He made through the blood of His cross is "not as the world giveth."[13] It is the peace of God and cometh only from Him through the One by Whom He supplies all our needs.[14] Look where you will and you will look in vain for peace apart from Christ. Search as you will for peace and your efforts will mock you unless you reach Calvary by faith. Fight for peace and your wounds will be worthless, your dying folly. Real peace comes from but one Source.

IT IS EXCEPTIONAL IN ITS CHARACTER. The peace which the Saviour made possible is not what the world speaks about, fights and dies for—an uncertain, unstable, unsatisfying something at which to grasp but never to be sure the grip is firm or lasting. No, it is something real, something restful, something refreshing. It is the sweet calm which enters a troubled soul after the battle against God has been voluntarily terminated and His terms accepted.

IT IS EXCELLENT IN ITS EXHILARATING EFFECT. It is the refreshing atmosphere of heaven inhaled by an exercised faith to clarify the temple of the Holy Spirit. It is the assurance of forgiven sins, the confidence of a present salvation and the certainty of future glory. It is the joy of a bestowed victory, the sweetness of a new relationship and the satisfaction of a new life. It is just as sure as Calvary,

---

[13]Ibid   [14]Phil. 4: 19

just as true as the Scriptures, just as unchanging as God,
just as eternal as eternity itself; yet, it is as free as the air
we breathe. God, who is rich in mercy according to the
love wherewith He has loved us, provided through Christ
a loving, living and lasting peace for all who will surrender
their wills to Him.

The Price—"The Blood"

For one to say that he has, or that he knows experi-
entially, the peace of God, presupposes conversion, justification, acceptance and inheritance. The involvements and
benefits are amazing, but they exacted a tremendous price.
The Apostle Peter recalled with much solemnity, "Ye were
not redeemed with corruptible things as silver and gold,
but with the precious blood of Christ."[15]

IT NECESSITATED HIS DESCENT. We must remember that
Jesus not only bought peace; He brought it. It is the peace
of heaven delivered to earth. It is the peace of God presented to men. Jesus had to come to bring it. Never shall
we know the humiliation this entailed. "Though he was
rich, yet for your sakes he became poor, that ye through
his poverty might be rich."[16] Nor can we assay the true
worth of such bestowed riches, for rich among them is the
sweet peace of God's love.

IT NECESSITATED HIS DENIAL. He must needs be rejected
of men. He made this fact clear. He must stand alone.
He must tread the winepress unaccompanied. He must fight
the battle without assistance. If man had contributed some
effort, it could never have been the perfect peace which
we know it to be. Whatever man does has the earmarks of
imperfection and the fingerprints of impurity. His denial
and rejection made Him solitary. It seems lamentable to
witness the sheep scattering when the Shepherd is being
smitten, but even this was part of the plan.

IT NECESSITATED HIS DENUNCIATION. He was bitterly
assailed by perjured testimony. He was called a perverter

[15]1 Pet. 1: 18, 19   [16]2 Cor. 8: 9

of the nation, a supplanter of the Roman emperor and a fictitious god. Through it all He remained silent. "When he was reviled, he reviled not again."[17] Even as His righteousness was tested in the wilderness, just so His peace was being tried before the court. Was He not proving the properties of His peace? Did He not demonstrate that it keeps the heart and mind? He was denounced with the bitterest indignities and the most blatant falsehoods, yet, as a sheep is dumb before its shearers, Jesus opened not His mouth. He had peace within while the turmoil raged without.

IT NECESSITATED HIS DEATH. The place where this sweet peace found its satisfying and sufficient release was, obviously, at the cross. Peace is irrefutably the product of Calvary. We may speak of His exemplary life, and it was all of that, singular in every conceivable respect, but it was the planted cross with the Saviour thereon that *struck the oil*. Many people, however, look upon Calvary much the same as undiscerning folk view rare art productions, utterly failing to see the fine qualities. Let us never forget it, the peace that we may know by faith in the Son of God, the peace that passes all understanding, was made through the blood of His cross.

The Place—"His Cross"

It was *our* cross, but He made it His own. It was intended for a malefactor, but the Master submitted to it to become our Benefactor.

THE PLACE OF FULFILMENT. The thunder of Sinai roared down the course of time, and the lightnings thereof, flashing through the murky mists of a decadent and discouraged Judaism, reached the proportions of an unprecedented storm at Calvary. The torrents of terrifying wrath poured down in incalculable volumes upon the dying form of Him Who was tasting death for all men. He was lashed to the tree by love, nor left it when challenged by the subtle

[17] 1 Pet. 2: 23

intrigue of enemy forces. He was hated, despised and forsaken as He wrestled in anguish unknown. The terrors of
the night hissed at Him, and the teeth of the Law gnashed,
yet He absorbed the stinging, stirring, death-dealing blasts
and became the end of the law for righteousness for all who
believe.

THE PLACE OF FINALITY. Said the Honourable Mr. Win-
ston Churchill of the gallant airforce in the Battle of Britain
during World War II, "Never have so many owed so much to
so few." He was thinking exclusively of the secular realm
and we shall not challenge the veracity of his eulogy, but
"I ofttimes wonder shall I know, how much I owe, how
much I owe. How much I owe for grace divine, how much
I owe that peace is mine." And one of the innumerable
wonders of the Cross is the glorious fact that what was
done there was done ONCE AND FOR ALL. Calvary need
not be repeated to replenish the supply of grace or to increase the flow of peace. Faith points its finger appreci-
atively to the Lamb of God and exults, "He made peace
through the blood of His cross!" This was the *shibboleth*
of the dying martyrs. Fastened to the stake and with the
fagots crackling and the flames scorching, the peace of God
settled with all the gentleness of the falling dew upon their
trusting hearts. And it satisfies today.

The finality of Calvary's accomplishments speaks of intensity, completeness and sufficiency. "Acquaint now thyself with Him and be at peace."[18]

---

[18]Job 22: 21

The Place of Propitiation

*"Whom God put forward as a propitiation
available to faith in virtue of His blood"*—
Romans 3:25 (Wey.).

WE ENTER NOW the *operating room* of the
Almighty. Those who witness the skill of a surgeon, as he
takes into his trained hands the preciousness of life, are required to dress in white gowns. One may go up to the very
door clothed in one's natural apparel, but when one enters,
the change must be made. Likewise, one may go to the
Cross in his tattered rags of self-righteousness, but to enter
into its deep and abounding mysteries, the white linen garments of the priest become an absolute prerequisite. Then
one may observe, with a quickening beat of the heart, something of this singular operation conceived by *Omniscient
Consultants.*

The text at hand gives to us a delicate yet delightful
slant on the developments at Calvary. It is not here the
viewpoint of the wrath of God outpouring but rather that
of the love of God overflowing. It is entirely apart from
the rumbling thunder and frightening flashes of lightning.
It is utterly undisturbed by the quaking, cracking, rock-
covered crest. It is a glittering gem which glistens on the
silver side of the dark clouds. It is the coloured footlight
on the inside of the curtain of darkness which dropped on
Calvary's scene. Our spirits are lured at once into the
sacred, solemn secrets which sweetly unfold to the discerning eye of faith. We gain sufficient boldness to step into
the three-hour period of darkness, only to find ourselves
surprisingly in the midst of a threefold illumination—the
light of love, the light of mercy, the light of grace—blend-

97

ing as a bow in the sky and betokening eternal blessing
against the grim background of excruciating suffering.

The Place of Divine Demonstration

THE SOVEREIGN SURGEON. "Whom God put forward,"
the Word declares. At once it is seen that God is the Divine
Agent in this whole significant matter. God gave His only
begotten Son. He put Him forward. He bound the Sacrifice with cords to the altar. "For God showed Him publicly
dying as a sacrifice."[1] "For God set Him before the world
to be a means of reconciliation."[2] It was a purposeful ex-
posure of the Son by the Father to the rigours of the Cross
and the ridicule of the critics, all with a view to redeeming
the rebels of Adam's race.

Abraham of old, in the offering of his only son, provides some pertinent illustrative material. We are reluc-
tant to term the beloved old patriarch a *type* of the Almighty,
but, in many ways, his experience with Isaac is illuminating
in the consideration of the Cross. There was a place and
Abraham saw it;[3] there was a purpose and he knew it;
there was a price and he met it. And when the appointed
time arrived, Abraham "bound Isaac his son, and laid him
on the altar upon the wood."[4] Perhaps this, though im-
mortally impressive, should be called an *adumbration*
instead of an illustration—just a faint shadow in contrast
to the Calvary experience. But the point is, it was the
Father Who offered His only Sòn. "It pleased the Lord to
bruise Him."[5] It was the Infinite, Eternal God who was
performing an operation at the Place of the Skull, in spite
of all that wicked men did in the display of their accelerated
animosity.

THE SUFFERING SAVIOUR. The Lamb of God was put
forward, put to grief and put to shame. These phases of the
Calvary operation, while converging in the one offering of
one Person for one purpose, are not to be construed as
synonymous. They were, respectively, the surrender of the

---

[1]Rom. 3: 25, Goodspeed   [2]20th Century   [3]Gen. 22: 4
[4]Gen. 22: 9   [5]Isa. 53: 10

Father, the suffering of the Son and the sorrow of the
Saviour. If the earth quaked, what about the reverberations in heaven? All hell was shaken. The graves began
to open. The Roman soldiers were seized with fear. The
Son of God was submerged in the caldron of pain. Nor do
we need to conjecture as to whether or not it was actual.
The Scriptures plainly state that "He suffered".[6] And it
was not a surface cauterizing by the heat of divine judgment; it was a deep, probing, piercing, penetration of the
impact of God's wrath. Remember, He was taking our
place. He was our substitute. What he had incurred, what
we deserved—the fierceness of holy venegeance—was the lot
which fell upon Him who died for us. The operation was
real; it was needful; it was successful. The corn of wheat
must fall into the ground and die in order to bring forth
much fruit.[7]

THE SUBLIME SIMILE. Why did God put forth His Son?
How was He put forth? He was put forth "as a propitiation". He was put forth "as a means of reconciliation". He
was bound to the altar, yet in a very true sense, He *was*
the altar. He *is* the altar. He is our *mercy seat*. That is,
what the altar was in symbol to the covenant people of old,
Christ is in substance to Christian people now. Thus, the
sublime simile changes to marvelous metaphor—then from
figure to fact. The putting forward as a propitiation was
the basis for and the beginning of our Lord's mediatorial
office, and there is but one. There is "one mediator between
God and men, the man Christ Jesus."[8]

We need not linger long at Calvary to see why this is
so. It was He, and only He, who was put forward by the
Father. It was He, and only He, who was acceptable to the
Father as a suitable substitute. It was He, and only He,
who was capable of finishing such a work. In a careful
confirmation of this fact, the beloved Apostle, assured, "And
he *is* the propitiation for our sins; and not for ours only,
but also for the sins of the whole world."[9] "Herein is love,"
he later added, "not that we loved God, but that He loved

[6]1 Pet. 3: 18   [7]Jno. 12: 24   [8]1 Tim. 2: 5   [9]1 Jno. 2: 2

us, and sent (put forward) his Son to be the propitiation
for our sins."[10]

The Place of Human Advantage

"Whom God put forward as a propitiation AVAILABLE
TO FAITH." When divine blessings have been brought
within reach of faith, heaven has bent very low indeed.
Yet, the Cross made heaven itself accessible to man. It has
made pardon, peace and the provisions of grace available.
When Jesus said, "It is to your advantage that I go away,"[11]
He had more in mind than His ascension to send the Comforter. Had Christ not died, the proffering Spirit would
have had nothing to present. Had Christ not died, the Comforter would have had no comfort to bring. Calvary has
given to us the advantages which are our heritage as believers through the Lord Jesus.

THE CALL OF THE CROSS IS CLEAR ENOUGH FOR THE EAR
OF FAITH TO HEAR. " 'Take up thy cross and follow Me,'
I hear the blessed Saviour call. How can I make a lesser
sacrifice, when Jesus gave His all." Until faith so hears
and so answers, the challenge has been missed utterly. The
initial call of the Cross is to the one dead in trespasses and
sins,[12] extending an invitation to receive life through
Christ's death. But it must be observed that, of the three
appearances of the word "propitiation" in the authorized
version, two are found in 1st John.[13] Here, the message is
to the Father's "little children," instructing them in the
things of the Spirit. But no one is well instructed in the
things of the Spirit who does not listen to the call of the
Cross. Nor does one go very far in Christian testimony and
service who does not avail himself of the continued advantage of the Cross.

THE WAY OF THE CROSS IS PLAIN ENOUGH FOR THE EYE
OF FAITH TO SEE. The direction of the Cross is found in
following the Crucified. The Cross, therefore, has given
to the believer the proper direction. The way of the Cross

---

[10] Jno. 4: 10   [11] Jno. 16: 7, Weymouth   [12] Eph. 2: 1   [13] 1 Jno. 2: 2; 4: 10

leads home. It is the way of blessing and fruitfulness. It is the way which our blessed Lord has prescribed for us. "If any man will come after me, let him deny himself and take up his cross and follow me."[14] Is this not clear? It is the voluntary way. It is the vital way. It is the victorious way. Nor is the Master pleased with our neglect of His instructions. "He that taketh not his cross and followeth after me is not worthy of me."[15] This reveals something of his heart in the matter. He opened the way for us, why then should He not be grieved when we deliberately ignore it?

THE POWER OF THE CROSS IS NEAR ENOUGH FOR THE HAND OF FAITH TO REACH. Ponder the truth involved here and your weak testimony will be transformed. Your spiritual anemia will give way to vigor and vitality; your faltering steps will grow steady and firm; while your fearful, fainting heart will become possessed of courage and boldness. What do we need more than the power of the Cross? We are, for the most part, mere pigmies in the faith, trying to grapple with principalities and powers and Goliaths of subversive forces. We try to justify our defeats, yet weep perennially because victory is seldom experienced. These are apostate days, we plead. Evil men and seducers are worse. It is more difficult in the 20th century to get a hearing. People are too much occupied with and diverted by modern inventions. Such are our feeble self-justifications. Do we mean to tell the crucified and living Saviour that the Cross has lost its power? The wisdom of our words has made the Cross of Christ of none effect.[16] But the Cross has not lost its power.

When we turn on an electric motor or an ordinary electric lamp, we are in no wise cognizant of the cost of the power at the source—the buildings, the machinery, the boilers, the furnaces, the planted poles, the strung wires, the skill, the labour and the staggering amounts of money invested. Sadly, but true, we are even less conscious of the unspeakable and incomparable cost of Calvary's power—

[14]Matt. 16: 24   [15]Matt. 10: 38   [16]1 Cor. 1: 17

spiritual power, divine power, power to enjoy forgiveness of sin, power to live in vital contact with the Infinite, power to serve in a global conquest against evil, power to proclaim a living message of eternal hope, power to pray, power to forgive, power to love. On and on *ad infinitum* the advantages of the Cross could be tabulated. And think of it, all we need, and more, to become fruitful, joyful, powerful ambassadors of the King is within the reach of faith, because Jesus died and rose again.

The Place of Infinite Virtue

When a quiet woman, longing for relief from a protracted ailment, reached out weakly and touched the hem of His garment, Jesus said that virtue had gone out of Him.[17] At the Cross, when a loving God, longing for the redemption of a race, let fall His smiting hand in judgment, how unknowable, and, therefore, how inexpressible, even inconceivable, was the virtue which went out of Him.

THE VIRTUE OF HIS WILLINGNESS. They "compelled" Simon of Cyrene to carry the Saviour's cross,[18] but nowhere along the *Via Dolorosa* was it necessary to force Jesus to the end of saving poor lost souls. It was voluntary. It became so in the council chambers of the Most High in eternity past,[19] was so when He left His throne in the glory and descended to this earth. It was ever so as, amid poverty and misunderstanding, amid conspiracy and enemy intrigue, He traversed the sands of time. It was His evident attitude in Gethsemane, at Gabbatha and finally at Golgotha. The nails could never have anchored His body. The Roman spearmen could never have kept Him on that brow of ignominy. It was His love. He was willing to meet the shame, to endure the agony and to suffer rejection, even of the Father.

THE VIRTUE OF HIS OBEDIENCE. The power of Jesus' full and unhesitating obedience ever and always makes a distinct contribution of its own to the challenge of the Cross.

---

[17]Mk. 5: 30   [18]Matt. 27: 32   [19]Psa. 85: 10

Calvary's sorrows and sufferings were the ultimate of His compliance with the Father's will. "He became obedient unto death, EVEN the death of the cross."[20]   Samuel was correct when he rebukingly reminded King Saul that "to obey is better than sacrifice."[21]   Obedience, however, may lead to extreme sacrifice. It was true of our Lord; it may be true of us. Obedience is productive of present blessing and prospective glory. Someone has fittingly said, "Go down the pathway of obedience and the Lord will meet you there." His own obedience is ever our great incentive and strong encouragement.

THE VIRTUE OF HIS BLOOD. "Whom God put forward as a propitiation available to faith in virtue of His Blood." What a message! Has the reader ever questioned the Apostle Paul's statement, "I determined not to know anything among you, save Jesus Christ, and Him crucified"?[22] If so, it would be profitably advisable to linger at the Cross. The message is exhaustless.

Faith is but a channel; it must have something to flow through it. Faith is but the hand of spiritual procurement; it must have something to grasp. The propitiation is available to faith and the directed exercise of faith lays hold upon the efficacy of the shed blood of Christ. Basically, we rest on the virtue of His blood and the veracity of His Word. This provides an unshakable foundation for faith.

We cannot find, in the ocean of inspired Revelation, greater depths to plumb than the virtue of the blood. Nor can we find a more profitable subject. The marching saints have echoed down the corridors of time their triumphant belief in the power of the precious blood of the lamb. Again and again we sing, "I know a fount where sins are washed away. I know a place where night is turned to day. Burdens are lifted; blind eyes made to see. There's a wonder working power in the blood of Calvary." And so there is. Every true conversion proves it.

---

[20]Phil. 2: 8   [21]1 Sam. 15: 22   [22]1 Cor. 2: 2

The Place of Preappointment

"This is the day which the Lord hath made."
—Psalm 118:24.

ONE SCARCELY ENTERS the portals of Holy Scripture until one is deeply conscious of the accuracy and the exactitude of the divine statements. Authority issues in specific utterances.

Here is a divine demonstrative. It marks out a day in God's wise and wonderful economy. Observe that it is singular, that there is only one such day. It is all well and good for men to say, time after time, when the sky is blue and the sun is shining in its strength and the atmosphere is most pleasing to their taste, "This is the day which the Lord hath made." This, however, is not the basic meaning of the text. The day herein referred to is a specific, special and significant day, the equal of which was never before, has not been since, nor indeed shall ever be.

Was it the day of creation when the morning stars sang their sweet refrain? No, as great as that day must have been, it is not the one in view. Was it the day when man, in the image of God, became a living soul in the beautiful paradise of indescribable splendor? No, that was not the day. Was it the day when a compassionate God broke the yoke of Egyptian bondage, thus releasing His sadly oppressed people? No, that cannot meet the description. Was it that day of miracle when Moses and his people were led through the Red Sea to escape certain defeat at the hands of the Egyptians? Moses sang joyfully about that day, but even it is not the one before us in the text. Was it the day the tabernacle was completed, when the glory

of God filled the place? No, this is not it, notwithstanding
the greatness of that occasion. Was it the trans-Jordanic
operation? What a wonderful day that must have been
following the long, arduous journey, to enter the land of
promise. But even this does not fit the picture. It must
have been the day of the dedication of the great temple
in all its entrancing beauty and spiritual meaning, when
the beloved king bowed down before his people in prayer
and gratitude to God. But not so. Surely then, it was the
day when, o'er the Judean hills, the angelic chorus sang
about the birth of the Saviour. No, as singular and passingly wonderful as that was, we believe it is not the great
day of days to which the Psalmist refers.

What day is this which the Holy Spirit so unerringly and
so specifically points out as the "red letter" day in the
calendar of the Almighty? What day could it be? Are
there any supporting and elucidating facts in the context
to identify this day which is prominent above all others
in the great and glorious plan and purpose of the Infinite?
There are many indeed!

Psalm 118 is related to the Passover. It is conceded to
be the last song which was sung at the paschal supper. The
context assures us that this is more than presumption. It
tells us about the "stone which the builders rejected."[1]
This is but an early preview of the cries which so greatly
perplexed Pilate outside the Roman judgment hall.
"Crucify Him!" came the tumultous demand. These were
the "builders." The Jewish people were the covenant
people of the Lord. Jesus came to His own[2] as the only
foundation[3] of hope, but was rejected. The Apostle Peter
said, "The Lord is gracious . . . a living stone, disallowed
indeed of men, but chosen of God, and precious."[4]

They sang also of binding the sacrifice unto the altar.[5]
But what sacrifice was bound to the altar? Abraham
bound his son Isaac and laid him on the altar;[6] but they
were not singing about Isaac. The import of the Psalm was

---

[1]Psalm 118: 22   [2]Jno. 1: 11   [3]1 Cor. 3: 11   [4]1 Pet. 2: 3, 4
[5]Psalm 118: 27   [6]Gen. 22: 9

not retrospective but prospective. It had to do with the fulfilment of the redemptive program. "The Lord is my strength and song, and is become my salvation," they confidently sang. "I will praise thee; for thou hast heard me, and art become my salvation." Surely these verses clearly identify this *day of days* in the prophecy of the Spirit of Truth. It was the day in which the blessed Son of God staggered beneath the Cross. It was the day in which the Lord of Glory was spit upon and smitten. It was the day in which Jesus was impaled upon the accursed tree. It was the day in which the Saviour sealed our deliverance with His blood. It was the day in which Christ was crucified. This, then, is *the day which the Lord hath made.*

The Day of Sovereign Design

THE NEED WAS ANTICIPATED. He who knows the end from the beginning knew what the rebel sons of Adam's race required above all else, and designed that, on a given day, such abounding necessities should be provided by God's perfect Lamb being bound to the altar of sacrifice. How pathetically blind are the great multitudes today! How completely have they overlooked their greatest need! There is a continual and concentrated rush for funds, fame, fun and folly in their accelerated plunge toward the gaping mouth of a waiting hell. Man's superb need is for salvation, and *that day* made it amazingly possible. "The dying thief rejoiced to see that Fountain in his day; and there may we, though vile as he, wash all our sins away."

THE DAY WAS AUTHORIZED. *Calvary Day* became Salvation Day for the whole wide-world. It was V-W Day for a lost humanity; and, as such, it was marked out in the economy of God before the world began. Weather conditions could make no difference. Even these features were pre-designed. It must thunder and lightning as at Sinai when the Law was given. The sun must go into mourning. The earth must reveal its shocking reactions. Nor could the enemy thwart the plans of Diety. He de-

ployed his forces in Bethlehem and the surrounding environs subsequent to the birth of Jesus, and with vicious
Herod in command sought to destroy the Saviour which
was born in the city of David.[7] He plagued each step of
our Lord's ministerial pathway—ambushing, setting
booby-traps and using saboteurs. He, himself, sought a
subtle defeat of Christ in the wilderness temptation. But
Jesus insisted in the presence of His disciples that "the
Son of man goeth AS IT IS WRITTEN of him."[8] The day
was set in the counsels of the Godhead .

THE DETAILS WERE OUTLINED. As a shining jewel stands
out on a black velvet setting, so this day shines forth against
the black background of earth's dark history. Jesus was
to grow up as a tender plant, as a root out of dry ground.[9]
In the whole of this parched scene of sin and shame and
sorrow, He alone among all the sons of men was spotless,
pure and undefiled. He was to be despised.[10] Who among
men was so much detested without cause? Of all the poor,
unfortunate malefactors who paid with their lives for
crime, the two who died with Jesus were the most favoured,
if for no other reason than that the fulness of the wrath
of man was vented upon the dying One on the center cross.
Jesus was hated and despised.

The Saviour was to be oppressed and afflicted,[11] and the
treatment He was accorded, even apart from the anguish
of the crucifixion, was excruciating. He was to be brought
as a lamb to the slaughter.[12] He was to be as speechless
as a sheep.[13] All of these details, and many more, including at least thirty-three specific prophecies, were minutely
fulfilled on the *day of all days.*

The Day of the Saviour's Doing

THE VOLUNTARY MISSION. There was no force exercised
to avoid the unspeakable humiliation which Christ knew
would be His inescapable portion. Concerning this day of
days, we read, "This is the Lord's doing; it is marvellous in

---

[7]Matt. 2: 16   [8]Matt. 26: 24   [9]Isa. 53: 2   [10]Isa. 53: 3
[11]Isa. 53: 7   [12]Ibid   [13]Ibid

our eyes."[14] Nothing is so crystal clear in the Scriptures as the fact of His voluntary submission. "It must have been wonderful love that sent Him from heaven above; to suffer for me upon Calvary's tree. It must have been wonderful love."

In the praying and preaching of our Lord, we gather many transcendently superb facts. He was, before His descent, enjoying glory with the Father.[15] He came to seek and to save that which is lost.[16] No man could take His life, but He would lay it down of Himself.[17] His willingness to do so much for us should capture our hearts, control our lives and compel our service. If love begets love, and it does, this will be the logical outcome in every one who has the love of Christ shed abroad in the heart by the Holy Spirit.[18]

THE VITAL MINISTRY. "The words that I speak unto you, they are spirit, and they are life."[19] And what were the words which our blessed Lord had just been speaking? "Except ye eat the flesh of the Son of man, and drink His blood, ye have no life in you."[20] What a profound utterance! Our finiteness limits our reach into the vital aspects of the crucifixion, but this we know, the flood-gates of life were opened there for a humanity which was dead in trespasses and sins.[21] When Jesus shed His precious blood on Calvary, He not only released an effectual flow but an abundant flood. Every life that taps the river of salvation by faith becomes a tributary supplied by the eternal, exhaustless *Source*. What the *day of days* made possible we cannot fully comprehend now, but of this we are sure, what He did there was absolutely essential for our everlasting welfare.

THE VISUAL MANIFESTATION. "And he that saw it bare record, and his record is true."[22] The Lord Jesus was put to an open shame. His death cannot be successfully gainsaid. Pilate knew it was He when he dictated the superscription to be placed on the cross above the Saviour's head.

---

[14]Psa. 118: 23 [15]Jno. 17: 5 [16]Luke 19: 10 [17]Jno. 10: 18 [18]Rom. 5: 5
[19]Jno. 6: 63 [20]Jno. 6: 53 [21]Eph. 2: 1 [22]Jno. 19: 35

The one malefactor knew it was He when he besought Him for gracious remembrance. The centurion knew it was He when he said, "Truly this was the Son of God." The women who were beholding from afar knew it was He. Joseph of Arimathaea knew it was He when he requested the body. Those who heard His tender prayer of forgiveness, knew it was He. He was the altogether lovely One ignominiously impaled between earth and sky. He was that day revealing the faithfulness of His purpose, the fulness of His Love and finality of His Sacrifice.

An Hindu priest once reputedly asked a Christian missionary to explain the basis of the Christian religion. When the missionary narrated the facts of Christ's death and His forgiving spirit, the Hindu priest said, "Get out of here! Get out of India! A message such as that will convert our people."

The Day of the Saint's Delight

THE INWARD REACTION. "We will rejoice."[23] Herein is a revealing fact. It means that the day of the Saviour's death made possible all real gladness and true rejoicing. It was this day which brought us peace with God. It was this day which laid the foundation for all prospective blessing. It was this day which opened heaven's portals invitingly to hopeless, earthly pilgrims who have no abiding city here. "O happy day, that fixed my choice on Thee, my Saviour and my God. Well may this glowing heart rejoice and tell its rapture all abroad." Even as it required His death to bring us life, it necessitated His sorrow to give us joy. And there is no exultancy comparable to the expressed satisfaction of knowing that sins are forgiven—that there is a oneness between the trusting heart of man and the loving heart of God.

THE OUTWARD EXPRESSION. "Be glad in it."[24] How can we be glad in the sufferings of another? Simply because, unlike all other sufferers, His pains of sorrow were designed to produce paeons of joy. The literal meaning of the word

[23]Psa. 118: 24   [24]Ibid

"gladness" is "springing about". It is the kind of blessing which puts a leaping propensity in the soul of man. When the ark of the covenant was returned to the house of the Lord in Jerusalem, king David was seen," leaping and dancing before the Lord."[25] Spiritual gladness is that exuberance of soul which acknowledges an inward work of the Spirit and outwardly indicates an appreciation. It does not always manifest itself in physical leaping, but abounding soul-pleasure is certain to be evident. "O the joy of this wondrous salvation, be our hearts all aglow. O, the joy! let the blessing run over and the joy overflow." The countenance of a believer should shine with Holy brightness.

THE UPWARD EXPECTATION. Perhaps the holy men of old were narrow-minded, but the early Church had but one celebration. It was the death of Christ—a commemoration of the *day of days*. Nor will it cease. When all the celebrations of men are forgotten forever, this day of days will be memorialized eternally, as people innumerable, of all tribes and kindreds in glorified array, clothed in spotless righteousness, sing their doxological hallelujah chorus. And to make it real and ever-blessed, the Lamb that was slain will be there. The One who was on the middle tree will then be in the midst of the throne. How can we help but rejoice and be glad in it, when we know that the day which the Lord hath made has brought us all our present blessing and future hope?

---

[25] 2 Sam. 6: 16

The Place of Predetermination

"Pontius Pilate, with the Gentiles, and the people of Israel, were gathered together, for to do whatsoever thy hand and thy counsel determined before to be done."—Acts 4:27, 28.

I**N THE PROPHETIC PICTURE**, a vivid colour is added to the subject of Calvary in the 85th Psalm which proves itself to be one of those productive gold mines in the mountain-range of redemptive truth.

If the frequent recurrence of a matter in a given portion of Scripture offers any interpretative value, then this little Psalm of some thirteen verses has as its general and glorious theme the matter of salvation. You will note, if you look carefully, that not only does the word salvation itself occur several times, but there are also such terms as deliverance and the forgiveness of sins.

The Plea of the Psalmist

Waxing bold in his confidence, the Psalmist laid a momentous appeal at the Throne of Grace. "Shew us thy mercy, O Lord, and grant us thy salvation,"[1] he prayed. The first part of his petition called for an explanation, the second for an experience. Then, with the utmost confidence of soul, assurance of heart, and expectancy of mind, he added. "I will hear what God the Lord will speak; for he will speak peace unto his people."[2]

Would it not be sad indeed if the heavens remained silent? Would it not be passingly sorrowful, even catastrophic, if heaven had never spoken? Ah, but heaven did

[1] Psalm 85: 7   [2] Psalm 85: 8

speak. The heavens reverberated with the announcement of the Most High: "Unto you is born this day in the city of David a Saviour, which is Christ the Lord."[3] But the text before us is prophetic. It was spoken before the coming of the Lord Jesus. Yet, with confidence and assurance, the Psalmist says, "I will hear". This is more than a promise of attention. It is the prediction of a response. But what did he expect to hear? What did he think the voice of the Lord would say? Statedly this, "He will speak peace unto his people."

The Response of the Lord

The reader of Psalm 85 cannot but note the change, a rather abrupt change, as he comes to verse 10. It is the beginning of the Lord's answer to His servant's petition— "Mercy and truth are met together; righteousness and peace have kissed." Without too much detail, let us allude briefly to some of the profound facts embodied in this statement. First, *mercy* stands for a personality; it is a personification. *Truth* likewise suggests a personality; it too is a personification. God the Father is the father of mercy, while Jesus is the truth. So, in the council of the Almighty, before the world began, the Father and the Son met together. Someone recently asked the writer if it were not possible to find three persons of the Godhead in the verse, suggesting that the Holy Spirit might have been the secretary of the council. We have no disapproval to register, for it is the blessed Holy Spirit who gives us the minutes of the meeting.

Mercy and *Truth* met in a conference more momentous by far than all the Casa Blanca, Teheran, and Potsdam meetings of world leaders. With them, the physical welfare of men for time was paramount; with the Godhead, the spiritual welfare of men for eternity was all-important. The council of the Almighty concerned not so much a bestial human usurper who had overrun helpless peoples of certain territories, but rather the arch-enemy of all man-

---

[3]Luke 2: 11

kind who had plunged the whole human family into sin
and despair.

The Considerations of the Council

It is not our desire to partake of forbidden fruit—to
trespass the bounds of granted privilege, for "the secret
things belong unto the Lord our God."[4] But there may be
a sense in which our sanctified thoughts may intrude into
this notable council. Never forget it, this meeting was
more than imaginary. It was actual. Mercy and Truth
met. They met for a purpose, because purpose is primary
and positive in divine procedure. Nor is it difficult to
ascertain some of the points on the agenda. Briefly stated,
the considerations were these: How can God be just and the
justifier of the ungodly? How can hell-bound sinners
become heaven-bound saints? How can alien men become
near ones? How can rebellious souls become reconciled
sons? These momentous matters posed a three-fold necessity. *First,* there must be a protection of God's inviolate
righteousness. *Second,* there must be a pursuance of God's
eternal purpose which he purposed in Christ. *Third,* there
must be an infinite provision for the satisfaction of man
and God.

The Purpose of the Cross

This world little knows, and, for the most part, cares
less about the true meaning of Calvary. The strong dis-
approbation of the Lord for sin is evidenced in His stern
denunciation of it by what He willingly did. The solemn
ultimatum was, "The soul that sinneth, it shall die." In
the preservation of the divine integrity, there can be no
revocation. The plan of God, at Calvary, was to supersede
this ultimatum by providing a suitable substitute for the
sinner, thereby vindicating the justice of God and making
possible an unconditional justification. It is said that God
can save, but cannot suffer, that man can suffer but cannot
save. A God-man could both suffer and save. Thus, God
became incarnate in the person of Jesus Christ. As man

[4]Deut. 29: 29

He could suffer in the stead of men, and this He willingly did. As God He could save, and this He graciously does. But there had to be a Calvary. Without the cup there would be no cure; without the cross there could be no crown.

Truth in the person of the Son had to do His work, that of paying the penalty for men. Righteousness in the person of the Father could claim the sinner if Truth would cancel his sin. Since the penalty for sin is death, then nothing short of death could satisfy the claim. Thus, Jesus came to redeem man, to pay the ransom price, to set him free from the law of sin and death. That is why there was a Calvary. It was God's way, through mercy, of meeting our need. The cross was not the crisis of Christ, but it is the basis of our blessings. Through His death, He is life for those dead in trespasses and sin. He is light for sin-darkened lives. He is love to replace the inbred enmity which humans evidence both for God and man.

The Agreement of the Council

Entering the council chambers of the Almighty to draw the blue-prints of human redemption were *Mercy* and *Truth*. Leaving the conference are *Righteousness* and *Peace*. Two different personalities? No, the same. Why then the different designations? Simply because God found a way to be merciful and yet retain His righteousness since *Truth* was willing to become our *Peace*. Finite thinking will never find a higher plane of spiritual consideration than this! Nor dare we overlook another delicately delightful suggestion which should at once lift all solemn hearts into the heavenlies of ecstacy. It is this, "Righteousness and Peace have kissed." The term means that there was thorough and absolute agreement in the plans that were laid. "Love found a way to redeem my soul; love found a way to make me whole." There was agreement! We were not advised of Mr. Stalin and Mr. Churchill kissing as they emerged from their several history-making conferences. There was not complete agreement with them, but the Father and the Son were at one in their purpose to save

a hopeless humanity. Of course, this is now gloriously con-
firmed by the thousands who, humble and nameless, have
found light and life and liberty in the provisions of the
Cross.

The Strategy of the Infinite

During World War II, the military strategists were
planning measures whereby the usurper, who was over-
running helpless peoples and destroying their free institu-
tions, might be defeated. It called for an invasion of his
territory. That was precisely the thought in the mind of
the omnipotent Godhead back in eternity past. John informs
us that "the whole world lieth in the wicked one."5 What
the invasion plan was for D-Day the world was not advised,
but what the divine strategy called for was part of the
explanation given to the Psalmist in answer to his request.

The realm overrun by the enemy must be invaded by
the Victor. But how was it to take place? The Lord could
have sent great companies from the glory with transcendent power, but He did not choose so to do. Instead, this
was the plan: "Truth shall spring out of the earth."6 This
was prophetic of the incarnation. "He shall grow up before
Him as a tender plant, and as a root out of dry ground."7
What an inauspicious invasion for a Mighty Victor! It
put a Branch in the manger, a Word on the cross, and a
Lamb on the throne. It did more than that, it put sinners
on the Rock. And what shall we say about the words, "And
righteousness shall look down from heaven?"8 It means
that God bends over the parapet of heaven, sees that humble
One who is hated and despised and rejected of men, and
says, "This is my beloved Son in whom I am well pleased."9
And mark you, this was at the time when the sacrificial
Lamb was being inspected for the altar of Calvary.

With the words, "And righteousness shall look down
from heaven," the answer to the extraordinary plea of the
Psalmist is concluded. These words are rich in theological
suggestions. It is likely that more was revealed than is

---

5 1 Jno. 5: 19   6 Psa. 85: 11   7 Isa. 53: 2   8 Psalm 85: 11   9 Matt. 17: 5

recorded, for there was a cross in the picture between verses
11 and 12. Between two lines we must find the weird yet
wonderful developments at the Place of the Skull where
wicked men did what the "counsel determined before to be
done."[10] Between these two verses we must see the blessed
Son of God grappling with the vicious enemy. We must
witness His unspeakable agony, and observe the unthinkable treatment meted out to Him. All this grim and gruesome experience was accepted in the considerations of
Mercy and Truth in their meeting in the inconceivable
past. God knew He must give His only begotten Son that
men might not perish but have everlasting life. The Son
knew that He must become a propitiation for our sins, and
not for ours only, but for the sins of the whole world.
Wonderful Saviour this!

The Grace of the Lord

"Yea, the Lord shall GIVE that which is good!"[11] the
Psalmist assured as he aroused himself from the staggering
revelation of God in response to his plea for an explanation
of divine mercy. Never before any expression like this!
Formerly, it was DO and thou shalt live. The rigorous demands of the law must be faced. But not so always. The
plans of the Infinite, which were minutely fulfilled, made
it possible for Paul to say, "Blotting out the handwriting
of ordinances that was against us, which was contrary to
us, and took it out of the way, nailing it to his cross."[12]
"Give" speaks of grace, for "He that spared not his own
Son, but delivered him up for us all, how shall he not with
him also freely GIVE us all things."[13]

The Psalmist in his joyous proclamation made it dis-
tinctly plain that the work of Calvary had to do not only
with GIVING but with GOING as well. "He shall set us
in the way of his steps,"[14] he assured. The Cross is, so to
speak, the switch which turns the human course from a
destination of eternal disaster to a way of eternal bliss. It

[10]Acts 4: 27, 28   [11]Psalm 85: 12   [12]Col. 2: 14   [13]Rom. 8: 32
[14]Psalm 85: 13

bridges the chasm between death and life. Its magnetic force translates the believing soul from the kingdom of darkness into the kingdom of God's dear Son.

"The way of His steps" is the path of the just that shineth more and more unto the perfect day. It is the way of truth and righteousness. It is the way of blessing and promise. It is the way that leads Home "whither the forerunner is for us entered, even Jesus,"[15]

All who meet the Christ of Calvary and own Him by faith find in Him full satisfaction for all the deep needs of life. He is the world's only Saviour, man's only hope, and God's only offer. All of this, and infinitely more than human minds can comprehend, was predetermined in the council of the Almighty when *Mercy* and *Truth* met together.

------

[15] Heb. 6: 20

The Place of Perpetuity

"When thou shalt make his soul an offering for sin . . . he shall prolong his days."—Isa. 53:10.

AT CALVARY all loss became gain. The inventory of the Cross produces some amazing discoveries. It reveals boundless and exhaustless stores of infinite blessings. The Cross established an outlet for the riches of glory, and placed the believer in vital contact with the source of supply. It is ever inspiring to hear a Christian sing, "Calvary covers it all—my past with its sin and shame. My guilt and despair, Jesus took on Him there, and Calvary covers it all." But this is only part of the story. Calvary covers the present as well as the past and has provided lavishly for the future, world without end.

Daniel was moved to prophecy that "after threescore and two weeks shall Messiah be cut off, but not for himself."[1] This is a clear-cut prediction of the sorrow, suffering and submission of the Saviour in a substitutionary manner, but the "cutting off" was never intended to convey the thought of termination. It was in a very real sense only the beginning.

Calvary Perpetuated His Purpose

Before all else, there was an eternal Father, an eternal Son, an eternal Spirit and an eternal purpose. The Godhead guaranteed the absolute fulfilment and the invincibility of this purpose. When Paul spoke about God abounding toward us in all wisdom and prudence in making known His purpose, he showed that it all stemmed from "redemption through his blood."[2] This is proved by the intro-

[1]Dan. 9: 26   [2]Eph. 1: 7

ductory word "wherein" of the following verse. The Cross, therefore, is the very heart of God's eternal purpose, the lightrays of which shine brightly down many avenues of illuminating truth.

NOW THERE IS AN EVERLASTING WAY. In one of his most impressive petitions, David implored, "Lead me in the way everlasting."[3] It is the way of light and love and liberty. It becomes personified in Christ, who assured, "I am the way, the truth, and the life."[4] It is the way of all comfort and assurance, the way of all blessing and joy, the way of all hope and prospect, the way of all mercy and grace. It is the new and living way. It is the way into which the gospel calls weary wanderers from the paths of sin. It is the way into which the Holy Spirit is ever seeking to turn men. It is the way in which the trailblazers of Truth have left their footprints of service and sacrifice on the sands of time to make rich our heritage and to challenge our hearts in devotion. It is the way of the Cross. It is the way which leads home.

NOW THERE IS AN EVERLASTING PRIESTHOOD. Aaron served well, but he is gone. His ministry has ended, but the Lord Jesus Christ, "because he continueth ever, hath an unchangeable priesthood . . . seeing he ever liveth to make intercession for them."[5] Let us never forget, it was only after His sacrificial offering, that He could or did become an High Priest. "For every high priest is ordained to offer gifts and sacrifices; wherefore it is of necessity that this man have somewhat also to offer."[6] And He has. He has everything to offer. This is the result of the completeness of His expiatory work at the Cross. Time and space would fail us in an attempted delineation of what He has to offer. We know that we have been bidden to come, for all things are now ready. As our High Priest, the Lord mediates to us, in superabundance, the provisions of His love.

NOW THERE IS AN EVERLASTING SALVATION. "But Israel shall be saved in the Lord with an everlasting salvation:

[3]Psa. 139: 24   [4]Jno. 14: 6   [5]Heb. 7: 24, 25   [6]Heb. 8: 3

ye shall not be ashamed nor confounded world without end."[7] Who is Israel's Saviour? Is he not the One Who was wounded for OUR transgressions and bruised for OUR iniquities? Is there any other Saviour? Let the Record answer with its own authority: "I, even I, am the Lord; and beside me there is no saviour."[8]

This announcement is potent, precious and penetrating. It indicates that there is something *exclusive* about the Lord. There is something *excelling* about His love. There is something *expulsive* about His light. There is something *exquisite* about His life. There is something *exceptional* about His language.

If, then, Israel may rejoice in an everlasting salvation, and if Israel's Saviour and our Saviour are one and the same, then may we rejoice in the same kind of salvation. However, we have more than a hope based on deductive reasoning. The New Testament abounds in amazing descriptives when setting forth the far-reaching effects of salvation through Christ—"Shall not come into condemnation;" "is passed from death to life;" "shall never perish." These are but a few bedrock assurances.

Now THERE IS AN EVERLASTING RIGHTEOUSNESS. For proof of this important fact, we could turn to many places in the Word. It is stamped all over the Sacred Page. The eighteenth stanza of the 119th Psalm is pitched in the very key of the point at hand. It is by no means in a minor chord that the Psalmist sings, "Thy righteousness is an everlasting righteousness."[9] The righteousness and the holiness of the Lord fall much in the same category of His essential attributes. If there is a theological distinction, it is in the sense that holiness pertains primarily to His inherent being, while righteousness characterizes His overt acts. Yet one depends upon the other. One cannot stand if the other falls.

We observe that the Lord staked His holiness on the integrity of His word when He declared, "Once have I sworn by my holiness that I will not lie . . ."[10] Thus when

[7]Isa. 45: 17   [8]Isa. 43: 11   [9]Psa. 119: 142   [10]Psa. 89: 35

He promised to put away sin by the death of Himself, this
He must do. He said, that He had come to save men, and
the only way of saving them was by the way of the Cross.
The Old Testament Scriptures set forth this truth prolific-
ally. Jesus also taught that He would be rejected and
killed. Had He not gone through the tortures of crucifixion, His word would have been proved untrue. His
holiness would have been undermined and His righteousness have ceased. Calvary was the place where His righteousness was not only proved but eternally perpetuated.

NOW THERE IS AN EVERLASTING KINGDOM. There is a vast
difference between a throne and a cross. The one is a place
of power; the other a place of punishment. The one exalts;
the other humiliates. The one speaks of dynasty; the other
of death. Yet, Jesus was crowned a Saviour as well as a
Sovereign. He "was made a little lower than the angels
for the suffering of death, crowned with glory and
honour."[11] How glory can come out of ignominy and
honour out of disgrace may not be understandable to us, but
the *dark room* of Calvary was developing transcendent
matters which time and eternity must reveal.

Glorious things of Him were spoken, and spoken long
ago, and it was promised that not one jot or tittle should
fail of fulfilment. Thus, Calvary could not interrupt the
divine economy. It was said, "Thy kingdom is an everlasting kingdom, and thy dominion endureth throughout
all generations."[12] When evil hands had done their worst
and all hell had conspired to destroy, the kingdom went on.
Why? Simply because the King Himself goes on. He is
the King Eternal. Death placed a firm grip upon Him and
registered an actual *knock out* blow, but the grave could not
hold its prey. The Roman court issued a specific command
to "make it as sure as ye can."[13] But He arose! An everlasting kingdom must have an eternal king.

The placing of the superscription over the Saviour's
head was not accidental. There was more meaning to it

[11]Heb. 2: 9   [12]Psa. 145: 13   [13]Mt. 27: 65

than mockery. "THIS IS JESUS THE KING OF THE JEWS," Pilate wrote. The chief priests and leaders of Jewry protested violently but on this point the Roman judge did not acquiesce to their wishes. Why? Because all the details were predetermined in the counsels of the Almighty, and this was one. Jesus was King. The prophesied kingdom-appearance of the King calls for wounds in His hands.[14] And of the very one who elicits surprise because of these wounds, it is said in the same prophecy, "And the Lord shall be king over all the earth."[15]

Calvary Perpetuated His Love

"The Lord hath appeared of old unto me, saying, Yea, I have loved thee with an everlasting love: therefore with lovingkindness have I drawn thee."[16]

CALVARY LOVE PROVIDES AN ETERNAL RELATIONSHIP. One of the brightest jewels in the Saviour's diadem of suffering is that of making possible the reconciliation of a sinner to God in an unending relationship. Because of the efficacy of His finished work, He saves to the uttermost.

> *"I've found a Friend, Oh, such a Friend!*
> *He loved me ere I knew Him;*
> *He drew me with the cords of love,*
> *And thus He bound me to Him.*
> *And round my heart still closely twine,*
> *Those ties which naught can sever;*
> *For I am His and He is mine*
> *For ever and forever."*

CALVARY LOVE PREPARES US AN ETERNAL HOME. "We have a building of God, an house not made with hands, eternal in the heavens."[17] If this be thought of as referring only to the incorruptible or immortal body of the individual believer, it still offers an infinite amount of hope and expectation. However, the Lord Jesus, addressing His despondent disciples, said to them collectively, "I go to prepare a place for you".[18] In either of these cases, and in all

---

[14]Zech. 13: 6   [15]Zech. 14: 9   [16]Jer. 31: 3   [17]2 Cor. 5: 1   [18]Jno. 14: 3

cases of eternal blessing, the Cross provides the possibility. These promises are to believers. Believers are those who have reposed implicit faith in the shed blood of God's Lamb who was sacrificed on Golgotha's brow. Without the blood, we would be without the blessings. Then, to further enhance our appreciation and gratitude, let it be said that the place now in preparation is for a prepared people. Calvary is the only satisfactory assurance of this. It is the blood that washes white as snow. It is the blood that makes us fit; and when it is once applied to the heart by faith, one is just as fit for heaven as ever one will be.

CALVARY LOVE PROMISES AN ETERNAL INHERITANCE. It is quite appropriate for the Apostle Peter to urge us to praise God for His abundant mercy when we know that He "hath begotten us again unto a living hope by the resurrection of Jesus Christ from the dead, to an inheritance incorruptible, and undefiled, and that fadeth not away, reserved in heaven."[19] This is very stimulating to the trusting heart, and it is as amazing as it is wonderful. The inheritance is incontestable, incorruptible, untarnishable, undiminishable, and non-transferrable. I know it is mine —forever. It will suffer no fluctuations with the rise and fall of the markets, no inflations with the unsteadiness of the monetary systems, no inroads by the cunning craftiness of astute but unprincipled swindlers, and no loss by virtue of intruding robbers. Calvary made this possible, friend.

CALVARY LOVE PRESENTS AN ETERNAL FELLOWSHIP. Those who walk in the light as He is in the light find that their fellowship IS with the Father and with the Son.[20] This gives something of the touch of heaven to our weary hearts here below. But there is something better—infinitely better. When taps have sounded and the activities of life's little day are done, the absolutely entrancing, breathtaking, heart-consuming experience awaiting all who love His appearing, is that of meeting Him in the air to "ever be with the Lord".[21] Here is food for our fondest fancies. Enoch walked and talked with God in intimate fellowship,

---

[19]1 Pet. 1: 4   [20]1 Jno. 1: 3   [21]1 Thes. 4: 17

but for a passing moment of time; we shall be with the Lord forever and a day. In Enoch's case it was communion, sweet and precious, in the Spirit. With us it will be fellowship, actual, visible and glorious. Again, as in every moment of lingering in the shadow of the Cross, we are brought to our faces in unutterable praise.

And what shall we say about the perpetuation of His glory? Any infraction of predicted truth in His. whole ministry, either actual or implied, would have stripped Him of His glory. And His wounds? They, too, were perpetuated at Calvary. The nails were driven not into the wood of the Cross alone, but into the fabric of eternity. And His exaltation? That also was perpetuated at Calvary. Those at that unsightly scene saw Him bent low; we shall see Him high and lifted up. They saw Him in the gruesomeness of His humiliation; we shall see Him in the grandeur of His exaltation. They saw Him upon the Cross; we shall see Him upon the Throne. His faithful, finished work at Calvary makes all of this possible, for He "became obedient unto death, even the death of the cross; WHEREFORE God hath also highly exalted Him."[22]

The perpetuating force of Calvary holds a marked practical value for the Christian. Lingering there keeps our hearts tender, our lives clean, our zeal strong, our devotion deep, our love genuine.

---

[22]Phil. 2: 9

The Place of Prospect

"He shall see of the travail of his soul, and shall be satisfied; by his knowledge shall my righteous servant justify many; for he shall bear their iniquities"—Isaiah 53:11.

THE VERSE BEFORE US is not so much an Alpine peak as it is a towering mountain range—a chain of lofty truths which cluster about the Cross of Calvary, elevating and magnifying the wonders of an incomparable love. But one does not reach the high places without climbing. A company of students from a Scottish university were one day scaling the heights of a high mountain. On their journey they were joined by a man who, too, had a desire to reach the summit. Scarcely more than half way up, the man said to the students as he sat upon a rock, "You fellows may go on; I'll just imagine I've reached the top." No one will be enthralled by the entrancing view which the top of the mountain affords if one goes but half way in his climbing and then rests upon his imagination.

We now have reached the climactic statement of this unrivalled revelation. The reader is asked to note carefully the four occurrences of the word "shall" in our text. They give to us clearly the homiletical divisions. But, in order to properly ascend to the utmost peak of this marvellous revelation, we must necessarily begin at the base of the mountain. Hence, we will observe the fourth *shall* first, proceeding successively in reverse order.

The Work of Substitution

"For he shall bear their iniquities." Here is the magnitude of Calvary. What the Son of God did, He did for others. And what He did for others was the most tremen-

129

dous, awe-inspiring, incalculable accomplishment of which
the world has ever had knowledge. He came to put away
sin. If we could trace sin in all its horrible and heinous
machinations and ramifications, following its slimy course
through the innumerable by-paths of its unspeakable developments, seeing its broken and bleeding wrecks strewn
along the highway of time, hearing the torturous cries of
writhing disillusionment, grief and remorse, we might begin to understand something of the infinite scope of His
undertaking. Then add to this the staggering fact of eternal
consequences—the blackness of darkness for ever, the lake
of fire, the endless non-satisfaction of inordinate cravings,
the inseparable association of "the abominable, and mur-
derers, and whoremongers, and sorcerers, and idolaters, and
all liars"[1] in an odious atmosphere of everlasting ungodliness. This is something of the pit into which iniquity pours,
and the sinner goes in the turbulent way of his sins except
he be rescued. Hence, the necessity of the Cross.

WHOSE INIQUITIES WERE BORNE? Certainly they were
not the Saviour's. Jesus was exonerated by heaven and
earth. The Father pronounced Him free of violence and
deceit. Pilate's wife testified that He was just. The Roman
judge declared that he found no fault in Him. The malefactor said that He had done nothing amiss. Thus, the
iniquities which He bore were not His own. He who gathered little children to His side was not the perpetrator of
evil deeds. He who taught the deep lessons about purity
of heart was not Himself possessed of evil thoughts. He
who was the true Bread of Heaven was without leaven.
No, they were not His iniquities.

BY WHOM WERE INIQUITIES BORNE? If we could circumscribe Christ, we could then circumvent the Cross. But
we cannot circumvent the Cross. For more than nineteen
hundred years, mountain-climbers of Truth have been
scaling this lofty peak of Infinite love displayed, only to be
lost in its surrounding wonders. In the Cross is an ocean
of love yet unrevealed, a mountain of power still unre-

---

[1]Rev. 21: 8

leased, and a sea of truth not yet fathomed; nevertheless, its love and power and truth ever flow freely in superabundant volumes to transform, strengthen and encourage. There is something utterly exhaustless about the provisions of Calvary.

And what is true of the Cross is even truer of the Christ. The creator is always greater than the thing created, and, in scriptural terminology, something was there being made. For instance, He made peace by the blood of His Cross. That which was made reflects the mightiness of the Maker. It was the Lord of Glory who came to deal with iniquities. He, becoming the Scapegoat, bore them into the wilderness of divine forgetfulness. On Him the Lord's lot fell, "and the goat shall bear upon him all their iniquities".[2] Once again the paradoxes appear with rugged prominence on this mountain of revelation. The Judge was judged; the Son became sin; and the paschal Lamb was equally the scapegoat. He was the great Creator in a mystical manner doing a new thing, and, while the feeble arms of our intellect cannot embrace Him, yet our weak, trusting hearts may receive Him. In full amazement we cannot but exclaim, "How Thou canst love me and be the God Thou art, is darkness to my intellect but sunshine to my heart."

FOR WHOM WERE INIQUITIES BORNE? Now we set our tripod to survey a dismal territory—the sphere of sinful men. It is never a pleasant consideration, nor often undertaken with any degree of thoroughness. Yet, Calvary would be better understood and more widely appreciated if men were to face squarely the almost indescribable character of sinfulness in the human family. Christ died the just for the unjust; He died the righteous for the unrighteous; He died the sinless for the sinful. He died for the Jews, in whom there was no soundness, but wounds and bruises and putrifying sores which had not been closed, neither bound up, nor mollified with ointment.[3] He died for the Gentiles, ever known as the heathen, those who danced around the golden calf and gloried in their shame. He died for the sins of the whole wide world.[4] Again we exclaim:

[2]Lev. 16: 22   [3]Isa. 1: 6   [4]1 John 2: 2

"Was it the nails, O Saviour, that held Thee to the tree?
  Nay, it was Thy love for me, for me;
 Oh, make me to understand it, Lord; help me to take it in,
  How Thou, the Holy One, could bear the creature's sin."

The Act of Justification

"My righteous servant shall justify many," saith the Almighty. And regardless of man's state of sinfulness or degree of guilt, Calvary has given Christ both the right and the power to clear His case before the bar of divine justice. Once I was under the wrath of God; now I am under the shelter of the Saviour. Once I faced the flood of judgment; now I am in the ark of safety.

WHO IS THE JUSTIFIER? He is the Father's servant; He is the Father's righteous servant; He is the Father's righteous servant who ever and always acts with wisdom. As He comes with portfolio from the Throne of heaven, it is with verified credentials: "Behold, my servant shall deal prudently".[5] But His death must precede His dealing. The Cross of Jesus answers the question, "How can God be just and the justifier of the ungodly?" The Justifier is none other than the Great Victor, who, acting in His right and power, bestows victory upon those for whom He substituted in death—that is, upon those who accept through faith the provisions thereof.

WHAT IS THE JUSTIFICATION? Justification is a basic factor in our "so great" salvation. It is defined as that act of the Lord by which the guilty are pronounced righteous, placing them in such a position before the court of heaven as though they had never sinned. This gives one, though an abject sinner, standing with a thrice-holy God. It gives one not only standing with God, but acceptance of Him and entrance into the family of the redeemed, a member of the household of faith. It makes the far ones near and the near ones dear. It introduces non-participants of the covenants to an heirship invaluable. This all sounds glori-

---

[5]Isa. 52: 13

ous, and indeed is, but the Saviour had to bear away our sins in order to make it possible.

WHO ARE THE JUSTIFIED? Before we attempt to identify or to characterize the ones justified, let us notice in the text that they are *many.* Why not all? Because, only to as many as received Him, gave He power to become the sons of God.[6] Was not His justifying work sufficient for all? More than ample, but few there are, comparatively, who sense their sinful plight and seize by faith upon their only hope.

The only subjects for justification are the ungodly.[7] Jesus came not to redeem the righteous but the unrighteous. He who is whole needeth not a physician. But, while there is none that is righteous, none that doeth good, all having sinned and come short of the glory of God, the majority of people go about to establish their own righteousness. Nothing hinders the work of justification more than the refusal of the guilty to plead his guilt. All who plead innocent allow no opportunity for pardon to be pronounced, or reconciliation to be effected. The great multitudes assume an attitude of *nulle contendere.* They do not commit themselves. But that is indifference of the worst sort. It falls in the category of self-righteousness, and Calvary means little or nothing to the self-righteous. On the other hand, where there is a realization of condition, the lost want to be found; the guilty desire to be forgiven; the sick long to be made whole; those sold under sin wish to be bought back; those who are unrighteous yearn to be clothed in His righteousness. These are the ones who, through the simple exercise of faith, through the instrumentality of the Word, are justified.

The State of Satisfaction

"He shall be satisfied." Satisfaction is that state of being which leaves nothing to be desired. While we sing, "It will be worth it all when we see Jesus", He sings, "It will be worth it all when I see them in My likeness."

6Jno. 1: 12   7Rom. 4: 5

HE SHALL BE SATISFIED WITH DEATH'S DEFEAT. His satisfaction speaks of the thoroughness of His accomplishment
at the Cross. The accompaniments of sin must be cancelled.
The dangers of sin must be dissipated. The victory of sin
must be reversed. Coincident with the initial sin came
death which passed upon all men.[8] It has been the black
plague which has draped bereavement about countless
hearts down the corridors of time, and, even today, every
funeral entourage carries weeping souls to the gaping grave
which but intensifies the sorrow. Death is despicable. It
is a shame to die, and this in spite of the statement, "Blessed
are the dead who die in the Lord". The only blessed feature about death for the saint is the fact that he is thereby
absent from his weak body and present with his wonderful
Lord. Shame attaches itself to death because death attaches itself to sin, and sin and shame are synonymous.

Calvary sounded grim death's death-knell. The full
execution will follow later in the plan of God. "The last
enemy that shall be destroyed is death."[9] What an in-
vincible enemy it has been, sweeping alike over prince and
commoner, rich and poor, young and old, Christian and
non-Christian. Every kind of health defence has been
thrown up against it, but it triumphs sooner or later, thrust-
ing forth its icy hand to grip the unsuspecting in its cold
and firm embrace. But the victory at Calvary makes Christ
the *Champion*, and He cannot be satisfied until this grim
monster has been overthrown utterly. That day is coming, and, as God Himself wipes away all tears from the
eyes of ransomed souls, the divine announcement will be
heard with resounding force, "There shall be no more death,
neither sorrow, nor crying!"[10]

HE SHALL BE SATISFIED WITH SATAN'S SUBJUGATION. The
Old Serpent is ever subtle. He dogs the pathway of man
constantly while his cohorts dig the pitfalls. He outwits
the wisest of men, then laughs at their debacles. We tell
him to desist but it does not deter him. We resist him but
he does not flee. We compromise with him and we lose.

---

[8]Rom. 5: 12   [9]1 Cor. 15: 26   [10]Rev. 21: 4

Surely the Lord Jesus only can "bind the strong man".[11]
This is precisely what He plans to do. The verdict, prophetically viewed, reads thus: "And he laid hold on the
dragon, that old serpent, which is the Devil, and Satan and
bound him a thousand years, and cast him into the bottom-
less pit."[12] True, he will be loosed for a little season after
a thousand years. Then comes his doom irretrievably. The
Seed of the woman has indeed bruised the serpent's head.
But the Saviour cannot be satisfied until the Devil's execution is complete and final. This assurance is rooted deeply
in the triumph of the middle tree at the place called Calvary.

HE SHALL BE SATISFIED WITH THE BRIDE'S BLESSINGS. The
Lord Jesus set His eyes upon His bride in eternity past.
Then, when the fullness of time had come, He descended
to give Himself for her. Now there flows from the Cross
the fountain of life to sustain her, the fullness of His favour
to encourage her, and pleasures at His right hand for her
eternal enjoyment.

(a) *The bride's blessings are pricelessly complete.* He
has blessed us with all spiritual blessings in heavenly
places. And this is but one isolated indication of the sweeping fulfilment of promised blessing. David, in singing about
the children of men who put their trust under the shadow
of His wings, exulted, "They shall be abundantly satisfied
with the fatness of thy house; and thou shalt make them
drink of the river of thy pleasures."[13] This is especially
true since Calvary's price was paid.

(b) *The bride's blessings are practicably abundant.*
"And God is able to make all grace abound toward you;
that ye, always having all sufficiency in all things, may
abound to every good work."[14] He lavishes upon us His
provisions, His protection and His power. "What more can
He say than to you He hath said, to you who for refuge to
Jesus have fled?" What more can He do? He sustains in
trial, succours in weakness, comforts in sorrow and lifts
tenderly when His own have fallen. Of the six meanings

---

[11]Matt. 12: 29   [12]Rev. 20: 2, 3   [13]Psa. 36: 8   [14]II Cor. 9: 8

which issue from the word *paraclete*, three pertain primarily to our blessed Lord. He is our Advocate; He is our Counsellor; and He is our Intercessor.

His precious promise, "Where even two or three are gathered in my name, there am I in the midst of them," falls in the same category with another stated encouragement. It is this, "Lo, I am with you alway." The former concerns our gathering unto Him; the latter relates to our going for Him. The one has to do with worship; the other with witness. The arrangement of their textual appearance is in keeping with the order of their true importance, for one must worship within the veil before one can witness without the camp. It is while we are waiting in His presence that we are definitely assured of His power; it is then that confidence accrues to act upon His commission.

(c) *The bride's blessings are prospectively glorious.* Since there is none among men to compare with our precious Lord, we would expect that in every respect He should be different. As He reached the climax of His high priestly prayer before turning His face toward the rigours and shame of the Cross, He might have asked some special reward of the Father for all His unspeakable suffering and sorrow. In a sense, He did, but not for Himself. "Father," He solemnly petitioned, "I will that they also, whom thou hast given me be with me where I am; that they may behold my glory, which thou hast given me."[15] This prayer, as all His prayers, will be answered. Calvary has made it certain.

The Time of Realization

"He shall see the travail of His soul." Now we have climbed to the very summit of the Calvary prospect. This 11th verse of Isaiah 53 epitomizes the whole message of the Cross, and the part of the verse now before us is the capstone of it all. Through the sorrow, He sees the joy; through the darkness, He sees the light; through the shame, He sees the honour.

---

[15]Jno. 17: 24

THE REDEEMED PRESENTED WITH SUPREME JOY. Tenny-
son, in his *Locksley Hall*, wrote, "I dipped into the future
far as human eye could see; saw the wonders of the world,
and the glories that should be." These wonders and glories
consisted of "Pilots of the purple twilight casting down their
costly bail". But the Holy Spirit dipped into the future
farther than human eye can see, and, through the Apostle
Jude, reveals this stirring truth: The Saviour is not only
able to keep us, but has the power to present us one day
faultless before the presence of His glory with exceeding
joy.[16] It is the day of the victory celebration. The ignominy
of Calvary will then be erased from His memory even as
the birth-pangs are forgotten by the mother in the joy of
her child.

THE REDEEMED PRESENTED AMID SUPERNAL SURPRISE.
There may be silence in heaven for the space of one-half
hour as the vials of divine wrath are poured out upon a
Christ-rejecting world, but there will be no silence as the
bridal procession marches down the golden streets of the
city four-square. All the celestial hosts will be awed with
evident wonderment as, concertedly, the surprise is expressed: "Who is this that cometh up from the wilderness,
leaning upon her beloved?"[17] The answer, of course, is
a wayward people won, a rebellious people redeemed, an
earthly people in heaven. Some from every tribe and nation will be there. Why? Because God gave His only
begotten Son for the world. Jesus died for all. They are
there because they have washed their garments in the blood
of the Lamb.

The suggestion here is overwhelming. The bride has
come up from the wilderness. Webster defines *wilderness*
as a confused mass. This is an apt characterization of this
world. But there is progress as indicated by the word
cometh. Step by step He leads His dear children along.
Some day the journey will have ended and the presentation will take place. He who brought us up out of an
horrible pit,[18] will not be satisfied until He has brought

16Jude 24   17S. of S. 8: 5   18Psalm 40: 2

us up out of this hateful world. And when He does, we will be in His company. Note the words, "leaning upon her beloved". This speaks of manifest dependence, mutual delight and marvellous endearment.

Yes, He who poured out His life amid the shame and sorrow of Calvary shall see the travail of His soul. At the Cross, it was grief; at the Throne it will be glory. At the Cross, it was pain; at the Throne it will be pleasure. At the Cross it was redemption; at the Throne it will be reception.

Calvary is the place of prospect.

The Place of Places

"He hath poured out his soul unto death"
—Isaiah 53:12.

I T WAS THE MASTER, not the malefactors, who
made Calvary immortal and inimitable. And, in thinking
of the Cross, we have in mind primarily the accomplishment of the Saviour. The Father now pours out His blessings because the Son then poured out His soul. The thought
of *lingering at Calvary* is but a suggestion for the grateful
heart to ponder more prayerfully and to think more serious-
ly upon the fact of our Lord's sacrificial work. Perhaps no
other spiritual exercise is so productive of deep and abounding gratitude.

Since the Cross became the spectrum which diffuses the
glory of God's love and the radiant energy of His grace,
and since the effectiveness of the Cross reaches to the most
remote corners of the earth with exhaustless potentiality,
it is to be expected that the values of Calvary are inestimable. This naturally follows since the operation was divine
in nature—infinite in plan and eternal in accomplishment.
The Lord of glory became "infleshed" in order to give His
body to the *altar of sacrifice*. It was from this bodily tent
that He poured out His soul. And just as the end of the
curse is the way of death,[1] even so the result of the Cross
is the means of life. There is grace upon grace and glory
to glory—an ever-widening radius of spiritual blessing.
The eye of faith may, in any moment of prayerful meditation, catch a glimpse of a beaming ray of blessed encouragement. When followed to its base, the origin is ever and
always Calvary. It is not only THE place, but the place

[1]Prov. 14: 12

139

of places—multiple in its designed purpose, manifold in its distinctive power, and multitudinous in its divine provisions.

The Place of Power

"And I, if I be lifted up from the earth, will draw all men unto me."[2] Here is a remarkable proof of the Saviour's impartiality—a guarantee that He is no respecter of persons.[3] It is not His will that any should perish, but that all should come to repentance.[4] Potentially, He is the Saviour of all men; effectually, unto them that believe.[5]

When Jesus said, "If I be lifted up", He did not use the "if" suppositionally. There was nothing hypothetical about His being lifted up. Nothing was clearer to Him than the inevitability of the accursed cross. "The Son of man must go as it is written," He had assured the disciples. What He was conveying here was the positiveness of a universal accomplishment. This was as certain as the fact of death. He came to die for the world. This He did. There was no limited sacrifice or partial offering about it. He draws all (all kinds of) men unto Himself—of every kindred, every tribe, and of every nation, from every corner of the earth. Regardless of the colour of the skin or the depth of the guilt or the language of the lips—He draws all.

It is interesting to gaze through the prophetic telescope and view future scenes. Gathered about the throne and around the Lamb are the once heterogeneous throngs, now homogenetic—standing in the likeness of their blessed Lord. There is but one answer to this—just one explanation. The crucified and risen Christ attracts all kinds of people to His loving heart, imparts to them His nature and integrates them into one body of which He is the glorious Head.

Nor is this the full picture. "All men" will not be in the glory—yet He is to draw ALL men unto Him—if not in love unto salvation, then in justice unto condemnation. ALL shall stand before Him. The prefatory "if" in the text

[2]Jno. 12: 32   [3]Rom. 2: 11   [4]11 Pet. 3: 9   [5]1 Tim. 4: 10

thus becomes clear. "*If* I be lifted up," He explained, "I will draw all men unto me." Calvary, then, does two things as inferred here. *First*, it assures His Saviourhood, permitting believers to stand before Him justified. *Second*, it confirms His judgeship, requiring unbelievers to stand before Him condemned.

The Place of Possibility

"When Jesus therefore had received the vinegar, he said, It is finished; and he bowed his head and gave up the ghost."[6]

Not until this moment could cruel death strike its final blow. It was ever the revealed desire of the Son of God to "finish His work".[7] Now, it is finished. Now it is possible for God to justify the ungodly. Now it is possible for perishing souls to be lifted from the miry clay and established upon a Rock. Now it is possible for Jews and Gentiles to drink into one Spirit,[8] for Christ in His death removed the middle wall—that otherwise insurmountable partition.[9] Now it is possible for non-participants of the covenants to become heirs of God and joint-heirs with Jesus Christ. Now it is possible for men to know the joy of sins forgiven. Now it is possible through faith in Christ, to call God our Father. Now it is possible to own a hope of glory and to sweetly and joyfully contemplate the blessings of eternity in the glorious presence of the Lord.

Now it is possible, as we journey where there is no abiding city, to anticipate an eternal home. Now it is possible, as we endure the piercing pains of grief, to expect a cloudless day where God Himself will dry all tears from our eyes. Now it is possible, as we witness change and decay, to hope for the time when we shall never grow old. Now it is possible, as we are plunged into the throes of heart-breaking bereavement, to have the assurance that the last enemy to be put under foot is despicable death. Calvary is the place where all joyful expectancy became hopefully possible.

----

[6]Jno. 19: 30   [7]Jno. 4: 34   [8]1 Cor. 12: 13   [9]Eph. 2: 14

The Place of Purging

"Wash me and I shall be whiter than snow."[10]   It is not always wise to follow man in our search for deeper spiritual experiences. Men ask amiss. They ask for blessings to be lavished upon their own lusts. Even some Bible prayers, while recorded by the Holy Spirit, were not necessarily of divine prompting. But David, with his broken heart and bitter tears, his humble confession and deep repentance, brings us at once before the Most High, into the very sanctuary of His blessed presence. The defilement of sin must receive cleansing, else there is a broken fellowship with the Lord. In David's case there was awareness concerning his sin and shame. There was evident sorrow in his confession of it. We notice his humbleness, earnestness and desire. A clean heart, a willing spirit, and a steadfast walk are needed by all Christians in a larger measure.

The redemptive programme is not only creative, constructive and corrective, but purgative as well. The Lord can make the foulest sinner clean. The leper said, "Make me clean". Jesus answered, "Be thou clean". The account states,[11] "He was cleansed". To His ancient, rebellious people, Jehovah entreatingly appealed, "Come now, and let us reason together, though your sins be as scarlet, they shall be as white as snow; though they be red like crimson, they shall be as (washed) wool."[12] For all such efficacy, the people of that day looked forward by faith to the effectual Sacrifice; we of our day look backward by faith, and Calvary becomes the focal point of our vision, the effectual means for our cleansing.

The time is coming when a cosmopolitan company will rejoice in a celestial celebration. Amid all the surprise prevailing, several facts will at once be discernible, namely, those in view are not where they were; neither are they what they were. When the question is put relative to their identity, the answer reveals that "these are they which came out of great tribulation, and have washed their robes,

---

[10]Psa. 51: 7   [11]Mark 1: 40-42   [12]Isa. 1: 18

and made them white in the blood of the Lamb."[13] **All**
who have white robes gained their righteousness on the
strength and merits of the cleansing blood of Christ which
was shed at Calvary.

The Place of Provision

"He that spared not his own son, but delivered him up
for us all, how shall he not with him also freely give us
all things."[14]

If you have ever wondered how widely the Cross of
Christ opened the storehouse of divine treasures, this marvellous revelation is the thrilling answer. Here we have
the Benefactor, the benefactions, and the beneficiaries. The
benefactions are not tabulated for the simple reason that
they are too numerous to be listed. They are too great for
us to comprehend. But the price is stated—God's Son delivered up. As a lad, the writer had a hopeful ambition
of becoming a merchant, of owning a store where he could
take from the shelves all that he desired without the painful requisite of paying for the same. In expressing this
ambition to the neighbourhood grocer, a friend of the
family, that childhood dream was abruptly terminated
when the kindly grocer explained that he had to pay for
everything on the shelves and in the wareroom. How
childish are we, likewise, to be unmindful of the incalculable price which was paid for our blessings.

God spared not His Son in order that He might give to
us unsparingly. The word *freely* does not mean without
price. Gratuity is embodied in the word *give*. To give
freely is to give lavishly, and this is how our Father is able
to give since the Lord Jesus covered the cost at the Cross.
It would be utterly impossible for an enlightened mind to
think of one necessary thing which has not been planned
for in the Divine Council and provided at the Place of the
Skull. This is the reason it can be said authoritatively that
"ye are complete in Him".[15] This enables the Christian
to confidently sing, "All that I need He will always be, all

---

[13]Rev. 7: 14   [14]Rom. 8: 32   [15]Col. 2: 10

that I need till His face I see. All that I need through eternity, Jesus is all I need."

The Place of Purpose

"Now once in the end of the world hath he appeared to put away sin by the sacrifice of himself."[16] As we sing the lovely songs about the Cross and celebrate with lilies and new apparel the fact of the resurrection, let us not lose sight of the fact that Jesus came to deal with sin. He will appear the second time apart from the sin question, but He came the first time to put it away. He was the only One who could. He was the One who *did*. The text tells us how. It was by the sacrifice of Himself. He is the Great Physician who can treat the cancer of sin which has polluted the bloodstream of the whole human family and dooms the undelivered to perdition.

The struggle was more actual and more terrible than the most discerning spiritual mind can begin to appreciate. Sin had not only perniciously engrained itself into the very nature of men but had separated them from God.[17] It permeated mankind with defilement, falsehood, perverseness, indifference, vanity, and mischief. Sin had left man without peace, without discernment, without righteousness, and without hope. This is the destructive *monster* whom Jesus came to put away. So satisfactorily did our Saviour succeed in His purpose that the Father assures us through the Spirit that, for His trusting children, their sins have been separated from them as far as the east is from the west, to be remembered against them no more forever. Also, that they are buried in the deepest sea. And where did Jesus sacrifice Himself? At Calvary.

The Place of Perception

Calvary has a remarkable effect upon vision. No one can see so clearly as the one who has first seen the Cross. Things are never so accurately viewed as when they are observed in the light of Calvary.

---

[16]Heb. 9: 26   [17]Isa. 59: 2

The religious Pharisees had just raised a series of questions. "Where is thy Father?"[18] they demanded of Jesus,
with no thought of believing the true answer. "Will he
kill himself?"[19] they querulously commented one to another
when Jesus told them He was going whither they could not
follow. And, touching upon the solemn thought of dying
in their sins, they revealed no perceptible understanding
of the matter at hand. It was then that the Master said
to them, "When ye have lifted up the Son of man, then
shall ye know that I am he."[20]

Jesus was here predicting that Calvary would prove His
deity—that, amid the shame and sorrow and apparent defeat, the Cross would make irrefutably clear that He was
the one He claimed to be. Perhaps these religionists did
not recall that, according to their Sacred Writings, it required a fiery furnace to prove the presence of the Lord at
a certain former time. "Lo, I see four men loose," said
the excited Nebuchadnezzar, "and the form of the fourth
is like the Son of God."[21] That furnace was heated seven
times hotter than usual, but Calvary was one thousand
times worse than any other death.

The Pharisees themselves, as indicated by the statement
of our Lord, would be instrumental in having Him crucified. "When YE have lifted up the Son of man," He said.
Yet through it, they would perceive that He was the divine
Son of God. No other so suffered. No other so forgave.
At no other crucifixion were the elements so disturbed and
the sky so darkened. At no other crucifixion did the hard-
ened Roman soldiers "fear greatly". Of no other did the
Roman guard say concertedly, "Truly this was the Son of
God". There is no record of deep repentance on the part
of the reactionary Pharisees, but they knew, as they stood
in the shadow of the Cross, that it was He. Calvary proved
it.

While visiting at our old homestead in the mountains
some years ago, our father shouted aloud, "See the geese
going over!" Mother, two sisters and I ran to the front

[18]Jno. 8: 19   [19]Jno. 8: 22   [20]Jno. 8: 28   [21]Dan. 3: 25

verandah, calling out, "Where?" "There!" replied Dad, pointing his finger excitedly toward the azure blue. But, at first, we could not see the flock of wild geese. Suddenly, one sister saw them with gleeful exclamation, but the others could not bring them into focus. We looked up the arm of our sister, with the disappointing confession that we could not see them. Finally, mother and our other sister caught sight of them, but the writer was still gazing in vain. In an attempt to be helpful Dad said, "Son, your chances are lessening all the while. Do you see that locust tree just below us?" An affirmative nod was given. "Well," he continued, "if you look over that tree, I believe you will be able to catch a glimpse of them." True enough, there they were, flying in ordered formation through the open heavens.

Many are failing to perceive the love, mercy and grace of a holy God as revealed at Calvary, simply because they are looking up the arm of some other's experience. For clear perception, we must look by way of the Tree that stood on Golgotha's brow. Then we shall have a clear vision. Then we, too, shall know that He is He — the gracious, tender, compassionate Saviour who loved us and gave Himself for us.

Let us *linger at Calvary*.

The Place of Poetic Portrayal

The Mockery of Christ

The One Who is in time to come
  To judge the quick and dead,
Stood once before the judgment bar
  And heard the verdict read:
"I find no fault in this just Man,"
  Said Pilate from the throne;
"The Roman law can't claim His life—
  Go judge Him by thine own."

But evil hearts the case did press,
  And clamored for His life;
Till Pilate scarce knew how to move
  To quell the growing strife.
He scourged the Christ and had the guards
  Affix a thorny crown;
And on His blessed human form
  They placed a purple gown.

"Behold the Man!" the judge announced,
  To waiting throngs outside;
"Behold your King!" he added then,
  As loud the crowds deride:
"We have no king but Caesar, sir!"
  The shouts at once ascend;
"And if thou dost not let Him die,
  Thou art not Caesar's friend."

The Roman judge perplexed and sad
  Sought then to wash his hands;
He gave Him to the multitudes
  To meet their strong demands.
They thrust Him forth to bear the cross,
  And out the gate to go;
Where Jesus died for all mankind,
  Because He loved us so.

I Followed the Saviour

In fancy I followed the Saviour,
  I travelled the path that He trod,
I found Him in faithful obedience,
  Fulfilling the sweet will of God.

I walked to the room where the supper
  For twelve and the Master was made;
I heard Him in sorrow inform them
  How soon He'd be rudely betrayed.

I listened to voices co-mingled
  In chanting the sad parting hymn;
I watched while the solemn procession
  Went forward by moonlight so dim.

They moved to the garden of sorrows,
  And three entered in with Him there;
Their eyelids grew heavy while watching,
  As Jesus was broken in prayer.

I entered the hall of His judgment,
  Where Pilate by Rome was enthroned;
How fierce were the cries for His bloodshed—
  The Saviour the world had disowned.

I followed Him next to Golgotha,
  But how can a human portray
The scene on the Mount of Redemption,
  Where sins were all carried that day.

I covered my eyes but the impact
  That came from the sight of the tree,
Deep humbled my soul in contrition,
  For there He was dying for me.

I'll linger at Calvary's mountain,
  I'll cherish the Lamb that was slain,
I'll serve Him with prayerful devotion,
  'Till heaven at last I shall gain.

One Must Go Free

The garden of sorrow, the shame of the morrow—
  What wonder His heart sadly broke;
He met with denial and then came to trial
  Where Roman austerity spoke.

The charge of His violence disturbed not His silence
 As mute as a sheep He stood by;
But the Jews found a clause in their volume of laws
  By which they demanded He die.

When Pilate had pressed Him and strongly addressed
      Him,
  And nothing of guilt could he see,
His wife firmly urged him not even to scourge Him,
  But rather to set this Man free.

He went out before them and sought to implore them
  To cease from their wicked design;
But his efforts were vain as they shouted again,
  And would not their desire resign.

He questioned the Saviour and watched His behaviour,
  And troubled in heart and in mind,
He weakly then turned to a custom he'd learned
  And in it his answer to find.

Barabbas was found and on no other ground
  Than a custom which Jewry decreed,
The Saviour was given to them who had striven—
  The robber by choice then was freed.

What Price Propitiation!

The rioting crowd reached the rocky crest,
  Where the rugged cross was placed;
And the rabble throng with their frenzied zest,
  The Master there disgraced.

The bulls of Bashan in wild stampede,
  Hurled taunts at the Holy One;
And the pangs of hell gat hold indeed
  Of the soul of God's dear Son.

The spittle of men on His bruised face,
  And the thorns pressed on His brow,
Were part of the cost of His wondrous grace
  Which flows like a river now.

The hardest to bear as we watch Him there,
  And search for the words to tell,
Was the heavy shame on His lovely name,
  As the sorrows on Him fell.

His followers fled from His lonely side,
  And none with a tear stood by;
The heavens were sealed, no help was revealed,
  Alone He must suffer and die.

How great is our loss without that dread cross,
  How dark would the future thus be!
But that which was done by God's holy Son,
  Gives hope to a sinner like me.

Put to Grief

At the place of the skull as the sky became dull,
  The Saviour at last was impaled;
The thief at His side began to deride,
  And joined with the throngs as he railed.

When the sign at His head the passersby read—
  "The Saviour and King of the Jews"
Their bitterness flowed as they danced in the road,
  And wagged with their head, "It's untrue."

The anguish of torture and loved ones' departure
  Increased in its mis'ry untold;
Then heaven recoiled while wicked hands toiled,
  And the pangs of all hell gat hold.

God put Him to grief for sinners' relief,
  And bruised Him with wrath from above;
He was smitten of God with the heaviest rod,
  And there proved the depth of His love.

They offered Him gall in the presence of all,
  His senses while there to confuse;
But He turned His dear head as He suffered and bled,
  And died as the King of the Jews.

But 'tis more than the Jews who need the Good News
  That sins can be washed all away;
So God put Him to grief for all our relief
  When Jesus so suffered that day.

The Incense of Calvary

'Mid the thunders of the darkness
  And the lightning's flashing flare;
As the earth rocked with the tremors,
  We may hear the Saviour's prayer.
'Mid the groanings of transgressors
  Who had no one else to care;
Then we find the Saviour lifting
  His dear heart to God in prayer.

As the crowds were milling, mocking,
  And their cries had filled the air,
Turning to their acts of violence—
  Then the Master turned to prayer.
"Oh, My Father! do forgive them,"
  Was the pleading on His part,
"For they know not what they're doing
  In the blindness of their heart."

When the tempest spent its fury,
  And the waves were at their height,
Jesus turned His eyes toward heaven
  In a darkness worse than night.
Then, as if the gates of glory
  Opened by a shining host,
Jesus ceased the painful struggle,
  Giving up at once the ghost.

"Father, now to Thee I offer
  My own spirit to Thy hands;
All My work I now have finished"—
  Having met the law's demands.
Thus His prayer was sweet as incense,
  Sacred to our hearts today;
He, the dying, praying Saviour
  Sweetly teaches us to pray.

What are the Wounds?

He sits on the Throne which is ever His own,
  And heavenly hosts He commands;
He gives us each hour His grace and His power—
  But what are the wounds in His hands?

He is coming some day in glorious array,
  To wield control of all lands,
With triumph assured through sufferings endured—
  But what are the wounds in His hands?

All kindreds shall wail, no foe shall prevail,
  As Victor on earth He then stands;
All war shall e'er cease as He proffers His peace—
  But what are the wounds in His hands?

From heaven to earth in lowliest birth,
  He came to loosen sin's bands;
He went to the Cross and suffered great loss,
  And there got the wounds in His hands.

He grappled with sorrow, no help could He borrow,
  Yet met all the legal demands;
He cried, "It is done!" as the vict'ry was won,
  But still has the wounds in His hands.

The price that He paid and the peace that He made,
  The whole of my life now commands;
But when heaven I gain, with the saints there to reign,
  He'll still have the wounds in His hands.

Pondering the Cross

How can I, such weakly creature,
Grasp the fact and trace each feature
    Of the greatness of God's grace?
Back across the years I wander,
To a mound so weird o'er yonder,
There to sit and long to ponder
    As a cross is put in place.

Something strangely grips my reason
As I hear them shouting, "Treason!"
    To the One on center tree;
Surely He Who there is dying,
Without once their charge denying—
Simply silently defying—
    Is the One Who died for me.

As I linger in my musing,
Cries around are all confusing,
    But the Cross its message gives;
As the heart in truth reveres Him,
Something in His death endears Him
To the one by faith who nears Him,
    And by substitution lives.

Let the world now quick observe it,
No one here could e'er deserve it,
    But He died for you and me;
To the Cross He went in kindness
'Mid men's wickedness and blindness,
That He might both seek and find us
    For Himself eternally.

The Day of Days

The day of days in the mind of God,
    As mentioned in His Book,
Is the one to which for peace and hope,
    The whole wide-world must look.

It was the day when from above,
    The throne of thrones divine,
Poured forth a wrath because of love
    For your poor soul and mine.

The darkened sky, the lightning flash,
    The quaking of the earth,
Were symbols weird, but clear enough,
    That hope was giving birth.

It was the day when hell conspired
    Its worst of acts to do;
And all its forces rushed on Christ,
    With pain to pierce Him through.

But on that day, oh, blessed thought!
    The One on center tree,
As true to God, salvation bought,
    To set the sinner free.

The Conquering Lamb

How great are the works of the Saviour,
  Surpassing the thoughts of mankind;
How deep are His wonderful counsels,
  How marvellous His mercy we find.
The heavens declareth His glory,
  The firmament showeth His strength,
But dying for poor, helpless mortals
  Is love that knoweth no length.

He sat on His throne in great power,
  And spake into being the earth;
He hung on the Cross in deep anguish
  To give unto men a new birth.
He met all the forces of evil
  Which struck the whole race like a flood;
He bore the fierce wrath of the tempest,
  O'ercoming it all with His blood.

The Cross proved the place of perception,
  Where men with eyes opened but dim,
Saluted the dear, dying Saviour,
  And solemnly recognized Him.
They said in their fears and their trembling,
  When once all their deeds had been done,
The One on the tree in the center
  Was truly the Father's dear Son.

He came from the excellent glory,
  He humbled Himself to the grave;
He trod all alone the dark winepress,
  But now He is mighty to save.
The Place, in the wisdom of heaven,
  Was plural in victories great;
The conquering, soon-coming Saviour
  Is ever the chief Potentate.

God, the Saviour Came

What condescending grace had He
Who left His throne that He might be
The Saviour of lost men like me!
   For thus He came to earth.
The glory of eternity
Was His to have and His to see,
For of the Godhead, one was He—
   How could He come to earth?

The cherubs flew with lightning speed,
His will to do; His Word to heed—
All heaven moved as He decreed.
   And yet He came to earth.
He formed the world and mapped its way,
He parted darkness from the day;
He boldly caused the waves to stay—
   And then He came to earth.

He flung the lights of heaven high
With brilliant glow throughout the sky,
The marvel of each passerby—
   'Twas He Who came to earth.
He made the man and loved him too;
The man then fell, and now how true
The need that he be born anew—
   So Jesus came to earth.

His entrance was by lowly birth
To find that man in all his mirth
Scarce knew the value or the worth
   Nor cared about His coming.
But yet He came, O matchless Name!
His peace to give, my soul to claim;
He wore man's flesh, but just the same
   'Twas God Who came to earth.